Jesus in Islām, Christianity and the Jewish Talmud

وَإِن مِّنْ أَهْلِ ٱلْكِتَٰبِ إِلَّا لَيُؤْمِنَنَّ بِهِۦ قَبْلَ مَوْتِهِۦ
وَيَوْمَ ٱلْقِيَٰمَةِ يَكُونُ عَلَيْهِمْ شَهِيدًا

And there is none from the People of the Scripture—[Jews and Christians]—but that he will surely believe in Jesus before his death [when he returns]. And on the Day of Resurrection he will be against them a witness. (Qurʾān 4:159)

Abū ʿIyāḍ
Amjad bin Muḥammad Rafīq
www.islamjesus.ws

Title: Jesus in Islām, Christianity and the Jewish Talmud
Author: Abū Iyāḍ Amjad bin Muḥammad Rafīq

2nd edition (4.1) - Rabīʿ al-Awwal 1438 / November 2018

http://www.islamjesus.ws

ISBN 13: 978-1-64007-359-3
ISBN 10: 1-64007-359-0

Published by:

Germantown Masjid
4944 Germantown Avenue
Philadelphia
PA 19144
United States

t. 215 848 2615
e. admin@germantownmasjid.com

Contents

Transliteration Table

Consonants

ء	ʾ	د	d	ض	ḍ	ك	k
ب	b	ذ	dh	ط	ṭ	ل	l
ت	t	ر	r	ظ	ẓ	م	m
ث	th	ز	z	ع	ʿ	ن	n
ج	j	س	s	غ	gh	هـ	h
ح	ḥ	ش	sh	ف	f	و	w
خ	kh	ص	ṣ	ق	q	ي	y

Vowels

Short	ـَ	a	ـِ	i	ـُ	u
Long	ـَا	ā	ـِي	ī	ـُو	ū
Dipthongs	ـَوْ	aw	ـَيْ	ay		

عَزَّوَجَلَّ	The Mighty and Majestic.
صَلَّىٱللَّهُعَلَيْهِوَسَلَّمَ	May Allāh make good mention of His Prophet in the highest company and grant him safety.
عَلَيْهِٱلسَّلَامُ	Peace be upon him.
عَلَيْهَاٱلسَّلَامُ	Peace be upon her.

Note: It is impossible to translate the Qurʾān into any other language whilst retaining its full range and depth of meaning. Hence, all verses from the Qurʾān cited in this work, whilst providing an accurate enough rendition of the basic meaning, remain limited due to the limitations of the English language and are unable to convey fully what is in the original Arabic.

Introduction

Jesus (عَلَيْهِ ٱلسَّلَامُ) Son of Mary (عَلَيْهَا ٱلسَّلَامُ) was from a line of Israelite Prophets sent to the Jews to proclaim the message of monotheism and to purify and confirm the law of Moses (عَلَيْهِ ٱلسَّلَامُ). The Children of Israel split into two: believers and disbelievers. The Jewish religious leaders rejected the message of Jesus who challenged their authority and rebuked them for their iniquities and excesses. The factions who believed in Jesus were of two groups: The very first believers were the "**Jewish Christians**" who were monotheists and kept the law. The other group, the **Pauline Christians**, exaggerated his status, deified him and worshipped him alongside Allāh.[1] On account of Pauline Christianity, the religious leaders of the disbelieving Jews vilified the character of Jesus (عَلَيْهِ ٱلسَّلَامُ) who is innocent of the excesses of the Christians and the unfounded claims of the religious leaders of the Jews. The conflict between Jews and Christians played out over the centuries and can be observed in the anti-Christian polemics in Talmudic literature and the anti-Jewish sentiment that Christian Europe retained into the 20th century.[2]

---

[1] The words, **īl**, **eloh**, **ilāh** and **Allāh** (the only true deity worthy of worship) are synonymous in Hebrew, Aramaic and Arabic.

[2] The writers of some of the Gospels were quite hostile to Judaism and the Jews and provided a basis for vehement attitudes in the early church. Centuries later, this developed into the idea that Jews had been replaced as the "chosen people" by the Christians and as such the continued existence of Judaism was an invalidation of Christianity. In the Middle Ages, Jews were expelled from numerous European cities and the Crusaders attacked Jews in German and French towns on their way to Jerusalem. Jews were also discriminated against following charges of "blood libel" and "host desecration". Increasingly, Jews were forced to convert or be expelled and were subject to torture and death, often by burning at the stake, such as what happened in the Roman Catholic Inquisitions from the 13th century onwards. Faced with persecution from Christendom, Jews sought refuge in Muslim lands, such as the Ottoman empire. In his lecture, "*How Islam Saved the Jews*", Jewish Professor David J. Wasserstein of Vanderbilt University, stated in a 2012 lecture, [and later published in the Jewish Chronicle as "*So, What Did the Muslims Do For the Jews?*"]: "Islam saved Jewry... Had Islam not come along, the conflict with Persia would have continued. The separation between western Judaism, that of Christendom, and Babylonian Judaism,

The Qurʾān and the Prophetic traditions make clear the correct position regarding Jesus to both of these groups—the "People of the Book" (*ahl al-kitāb*)—in their disputes with each other: One failed to act by the truth when it came to them and rejected the message of Jesus out of pride and arrogance. The other acted upon ignorance—thereby abandoning and opposing authentic revealed knowledge—and fell into exaggeration by deifying him and worshipping him alongside Allāh. Both of these groups were guilty of excesses and exaggeration in religion as well as **alteration** (*tabdīl*), **distortion** (*taḥrīf*) and **concealment** (*kitmān*) of the Book. This is something the Qurʾān rehearses to them and which the learned amongst their priests and historians know to be factual reality as they are well aware of the deeds of their predecessors in taking liberties with scripture. Allāh (عَزَّوَجَلَّ) stated:

يَٰٓأَهْلَ ٱلْكِتَٰبِ لَا تَغْلُوا۟ فِى دِينِكُمْ وَلَا تَقُولُوا۟ عَلَى ٱللَّهِ إِلَّا ٱلْحَقَّ

"O People of the Scripture, do not commit excess in your religion and nor say about Allāh except the truth." (4:171).

---

that of Mesopotamia, would have intensified. Jewry in the west would have declined to disappearance in many areas. And Jewry in the east would have become just another oriental cult. But this was all prevented by the rise of Islam. The Islamic conquests of the seventh century changed the world, and did so with dramatic, wide-ranging and permanent effect for the Jews. Within a century of the death of Mohammad, in 632, Muslim armies had conquered almost the whole of the world where Jews lived, from Spain eastward across North Africa and the Middle East as far as the eastern frontier of Iran and beyond. Almost all the Jews in the world were now ruled by Islam. This new situation transformed Jewish existence. Their fortunes changed in legal, demographic, social, religious, political, geographical, economic, linguistic and cultural terms - all for the better." The Jewish Chronicle, 24 May 2012 (online). This is not to say that Jews never suffered any oppression at the hands of unjust Muslim rulers at all, but overwhelmingly, they fared much better in the Muslim lands. For more details one can refer to "*A History of the Jewish People*" edited by Haim Hillel Ben-Sasson, Harvard University Press (1985). It is a comprehensive book written by six Jewish scholars from Hebrew University in Jerusalem for Jewish readers and spans 5000 years of history. A consistent pattern emerges from the book that throughout Islāmic history Jews have fared well and lived in comfortable conditions.

Regarding their alteration (*tabdīl*):

فَوَيْلٌ لِّلَّذِينَ يَكْتُبُونَ ٱلْكِتَٰبَ بِأَيْدِيهِمْ ثُمَّ يَقُولُونَ هَٰذَا مِنْ عِندِ ٱللَّهِ لِيَشْتَرُوا۟ بِهِۦ ثَمَنًا قَلِيلًا فَوَيْلٌ لَّهُم مِّمَّا كَتَبَتْ أَيْدِيهِمْ وَوَيْلٌ لَّهُم مِّمَّا يَكْسِبُونَ

"So woe to those who write the 'scripture' with their own hands, then say, 'This is from Allāh' in order to exchange it for a small price. Woe to them for what their hands have written and woe to them for what they earn thereby." (2:79).

Regarding their distortion (*taḥrīf*):

أَفَتَطْمَعُونَ أَن يُؤْمِنُوا۟ لَكُمْ وَقَدْ كَانَ فَرِيقٌ مِّنْهُمْ يَسْمَعُونَ كَلَٰمَ ٱللَّهِ ثُمَّ يُحَرِّفُونَهُۥ مِنۢ بَعْدِ مَا عَقَلُوهُ وَهُمْ يَعْلَمُونَ

"Do you covet [the hope, O believers], that they would believe [in Islām] while a party of them used to hear the words of Allāh and then distort [the Torah] after they had understood it while they had knowledge [of what they were doing]?" (2:75).

Regarding their concealment (*kitmān*):

يَٰٓأَهْلَ ٱلْكِتَٰبِ لِمَ تَلْبِسُونَ ٱلْحَقَّ بِٱلْبَٰطِلِ وَتَكْتُمُونَ ٱلْحَقَّ وَأَنتُمْ تَعْلَمُونَ

"O People of the Scripture, why do you confuse the truth with falsehood and conceal the truth while you know [it]?" (3:71).

Muḥammad (صَلَّى ٱللَّهُ عَلَيْهِ وَسَلَّمَ) invited the Jews and Christians to the truth which they had abandoned, altered or concealed and debated with them regarding matters of divinity, scripture, law and the status of Jesus the Messiah. They were convinced that he was indeed a genuine Prophet because he was mentioned in their scriptures by name as מהמד "Muḥammad" and also אחמד "Aḥmad" and they recognised his qualities and actions: An **illiterate prophet** from the offspring of **Kedar** (son of Ishmael) who would appear from the deserts of **Paran** (Mecca). He would be expelled from his city and migrate to **Mount Sela** (Madīnah), which would sing his praise upon his arrival and glorify the Lord. He would then return with ten thousand of his companions, **victorious against the idolaters** without battle and would **come with a law**. His qualities and the major events of his life were mentioned in their scripture as well as the descriptions of his followers and their rituals and rites. Some of the Jews accepted Islām, as did many Christians.

However, others rejected him and his message on grounds of pride and concealed the truth knowingly.

Allāh (عَزَّوَجَلَّ) said:

ٱلَّذِينَ ءَاتَيْنَٰهُمُ ٱلْكِتَٰبَ يَعْرِفُونَهُۥ كَمَا يَعْرِفُونَ أَبْنَآءَهُمْ وَإِنَّ فَرِيقًا مِّنْهُمْ لَيَكْتُمُونَ ٱلْحَقَّ وَهُمْ يَعْلَمُونَ

"Those to whom We gave the Scripture [Jews and Christians] know him [Muḥammad] as they know their own sons. But indeed, a party of them conceal the truth while they know [it]." (2:146).

Jesus the Messiah holds a lofty and honourable position in Islām as does his righteous and chaste mother, Mary (عَلَيْهَاٱلسَّلَامُ). Muslims do not tolerate denigration of any of the Prophets and Messengers and especially the five resolute Messengers: Noah, Abraham, Moses, Jesus (عَلَيْهِمُٱلسَّلَامُ) and Muḥammad (صَلَّىٱللَّهُعَلَيْهِوَسَلَّمَ).

As for the negative portrayal of the Prophets of Allāh in the Torah and the ascription of reprehensible deeds to them, it is all from the fabrications of the poisoned pens of the scribes. All the Prophets and Messengers were noble, upright, righteous men. They were infallible in matters of revelation and its conveyance. They were secure (*maʿṣūm*) from falling into major sin. As for minor sins (errors), the Prophets may fall into them, but they do not persist upon them after being notified by Allāh and repenting. Further, Prophets and Messengers have a much higher standard of uprightness in character than those besides them. Thus, their "minor sins" may consist of mistakes and errors in judgement—such as choosing the least beneficial of two beneficial options—for which an ordinary person would not be subject to blame. This is the Islāmic position regarding the status of the Prophets and Messengers.

In what follows we present the treatment of Jesus within Christianity, the Jewish Talmud and Islām following a brief primer on the monotheism of the Prophets.

The Monotheism of the Prophets

The Prophets and Messengers invited people to worship Allāh alone by appealing to their in-built natural disposition known as the **fiṭrah**. Every child is born with this faculty in which there is an imprint of the existence of a creator as well as a basic moral sense of right and wrong. If left alone without any contrary teaching the child will grow up desiring and wanting to be grateful to its Creator for all the favours he or she enjoys on a daily basis and for the evident signs that are observed in both the horizons and the souls. Any idea or belief that causes a person to deviate from this innate default is unnatural, speculative and clashes with what is empirically known through the physical senses and basic reason. Such ideas and the deviations from innate disposition arising from them are addressed by **arguments of reason** alluded to in **revealed knowledge**.

Thus, all three—*innate disposition* (**fiṭrah**), *sound reason* (**'aql ṣarīḥ**) and *authentic revelation* (**naql saḥīḥ**)—point to worship of the sole creator and one true deity, Allāh, as being the truth and justice upon which the Heavens and Earth are created and persist. Multiplicities, triads and trinities are external and foreign to intuition, reason and revelation. *Innate disposition*—or intuition—rejects worship of multiple deities. *Sound reason* rejects multiple deities and the worship of that which is created and needy. *Authentic revelation* confirms what agrees with innate disposition and sound reason. There is no conflict between authentic revelation, sound reason and unchanged innate disposition. Conflict arises when innate disposition is corrupted through contrary teaching or when false, incoherent reasoning is applied [one in three; three in one; God is human; human is God; all at the same time] or when revelation is corrupted by alteration, insertion and misinterpretation.

Confirming that all of His Messengers were sent with this simple message of pure monotheism, Allāh (عَزَّوَجَلَّ) said:

وَمَآ أَرْسَلْنَا مِن قَبْلِكَ مِن رَّسُولٍ إِلَّا نُوحِىٓ إِلَيْهِ أَنَّهُۥ لَآ إِلَٰهَ إِلَّآ أَنَا۠ فَٱعْبُدُونِ

"And We sent not before you any messenger except that We revealed to him [to proclaim] that, 'There is no deity except Me, so worship Me [alone]'." (21:25).

Allāh (عَزَّوَجَلَّ) also said:

وَلَقَدْ بَعَثْنَا فِى كُلِّ أُمَّةٍ رَّسُولًا أَنِ ٱعْبُدُوا۟ ٱللَّهَ وَٱجْتَنِبُوا۟ ٱلطَّٰغُوتَ

"And We certainly sent into every nation a messenger, [saying], 'Worship Allāh and [alone] shun false deities'." (16:36).

And Allāh (عَزَّوَجَلَّ) also said:

وَإِنَّ ٱللَّهَ رَبِّى وَرَبُّكُمْ فَٱعْبُدُوهُ هَٰذَا صِرَٰطٌ مُّسْتَقِيمٌ

"[Jesus said], 'And indeed, Allāh is my Lord and your Lord, so worship Him [alone]. That is a straight path'." (19:36).

The **Monotheism (Tawḥīd)** which all of the Prophets called to is not merely to believe in one creator, provider and sustainer because this is already rooted in innate disposition. Every child is born with this predisposition and it is referred to as the *fiṭrah* as has preceded.

Rather, the monotheism of the Prophets it is to exclusively single out this creator, Allāh, with all forms and types of worship.

These forms and types include love (*maḥabbah*), fear (*khawf*), hope (*rajāʾ*), reliance (*tawakkul*), bowing (*sujūd*), prostration (*rukūʿ*), prayer (*ṣālāt*), invocation (*duʿā*), seeking aid (*istiʿānah*) and soliciting rescue (*istighāthah*) by way of example and include both what is inward (the heart, its belief and its feelings, emotions and states) and what is outward (the tongue and the limbs, utterances and deeds). Thus, claiming to believe in one Creator and one God whilst directing these forms and types of worship to others, be they angels, prophets, saints [pious men whether dead or alive], stones, trees, idols, the sun, moon and stars or any of the elements, forces or intertwined ways and means and causes and effects is a contradiction.

One cannot claim to believe that only God creates, provides, sustains, controls, regulates, gives and takes, and then offer worship to what is created, temporal and in need. It is a violation of reason, comprises the greatest injustice and represents the height of folly and shallowness in intellect.

The Islāmic message of all the Prophets is built upon two mighty foundations: **Firstly**: That Allāh is exclusively worshipped alone, no partners are associated with Him in worship and all deities besides Him are shunned. **Secondly**: That He is not worshipped except through what He legislated and commanded. The message of the

Prophets combines between these two with the second being a means of fulfilment for the first.[3]

The Jews and Christians swerved from these foundations. They worshipped others besides Allāh and altered, distorted, abrogated or, in the case of the Christians, did away with the law altogether and worshipped Allāh through their own innovations and whatever they absorbed of the rituals of the Pagans.

Acts of worship are founded upon the principles of legislation (*sharʿ*) and faithful observance (*ittibāʿ*) which is imitation of the Messengers of Allāh in what they conveyed of the law. It is not for anyone to worship Allāh except through what His Messengers enjoined of both obligatory and recommended deeds. Allāh is not worshipped through affairs for which He gave no authority. Thus every act of worship must be founded upon pure monotheistic belief, be directed only to Allāh, done sincerely for His sake, and done in compliance with what has been legislated.

This is the way of Abraham, Isaac, Ishmael, Jacob, Moses, David, Solomon, the Israelite prophets, Jesus and Muḥammad (صَلَّىٰ ٱللَّٰهُ عَلَيْهِ وَسَلَّمَ).

The treatment of monotheism in the Qurʾān and the Prophetic traditions is vast, comprehensive and complete. It is a completion and perfection of the message of all of the Prophets. The Prophet Muḥammad (صَلَّىٰ ٱللَّٰهُ عَلَيْهِ وَسَلَّمَ) said, "*Both in this world and in the Hereafter, I am the nearest of all the people to Jesus, the son of Mary. The prophets are paternal brothers, their mothers are different, but their religion is one.*"[4] Traces of this message of Islām can still be found in what remains of the Torah and the Gospel. In Deuteronomy 6:4 we find: "Hear O Israel, the Lord our God, the Lord is one." In Zechariah 14:9: "On that day there will be [but] one Lord and His name will be the One". And in Mark 12:29: "'The most important one,' answered Jesus, 'is this: 'Hear, O Israel: The Lord our God, the Lord is one'." The meaning is

---

[3] In Islām, whilst deeds are essential to faith and are required for salvation, none will enter Paradise except through the grace, mercy and forgiveness of Allāh. This is because Allāh is the one who created and gave man abilities and strengths to act, sent him guidance, granted him success in following it, and overlooked his sins and shortcomings.

[4] Related by Imām al-Bukhārī in his compilation of Prophetic traditions.

lost in translation,[5] but these statements, in the original Hebrew or Aramaic יְהוָה אֱלֹהֵינוּ, יְהוָה אֶחָד *'eloheynu yahúwah 'echad*[6] and יְהוָה אֶחָד וּשְׁמוֹ אֶחָד *yahúwah 'echad ush'mo 'echad*[7] are identical to the statement **ilāhunā aḥād**, "Our Deity is uniquely one" and **qul huwallāhu aḥad**, "Say: He is Allāh [who is] Uniquely One" and the declaration of monotheism in Islām, **lā ilāha illallāh,** which means: "No deity *deserves* or *has the right to be worshipped* but Allāh alone."[8]

We also read in Matthew, "Again, the devil took him to a very high mountain and showed Him all the kingdoms of the world and their glory. 'All this I will give You', he said, 'if You will fall down and worship me.' 'Away from me, Satan!' Jesus declared. 'For it is written: '*Worship the Lord your God and serve Him only*'.'"[9]

Islām is founded upon this monotheism and upon submission to the will of Allāh, just as Jesus himself taught in what is ascribed to him and whose meaning the Qurʾān corroborates. Jesus said: "Not everyone who says to me, 'Lord, Lord,' will enter the kingdom of heaven, but only the one who does the will of my Father in heaven.[10] On that day many will say to me, 'Lord, Lord, did we not prophesy in your name, and cast out demons in your name, and do many deeds of

---

[5] The words *īl*, *eloh*, *ilāh* refer not to a mere creator, lord, but to a deity to whom longing and devotion are shown. Thus, deities are many and varied. The meaning of these statements of monotheism, as originally intended in all revealed books is that nothing has the right to be worshipped in truth but Allāh alone and whatever is worshipped besides Allāh is worshipped in falsehood. This is the meaning of the simple statement (لا إله إلا الله), *lā ilāha illallāh*. It is often incorrectly translated as "There is no god but God" which corrupts the meaning, or "There is no supreme creator but God" which is a deficient translation that eliminates the essence of the meaning.

[6] Meaning: Our deity (*ilāhunā*), the Lord, is one (*aḥad*).

[7] Meaning: The Lord is one (*aḥad*), His Name (*ism*) is One (*aḥad*).

[8] The translation, "There is no god but God" is erroneous and lacks the essence of the meaning since there are many gods in existence.

[9] Matthew 4:8-10.

[10] Submission to Allāh's will (which means obeying Him in compliance with His command, upon a pure and strict monotheistic belief) is the meaning of "Islām" and this is what Jesus and all the Prophets called to. It is a simple message devoid of mystery, conflict, confusion and contradiction and is instantly agreeable to intuition and innate disposition.

power in your name?' Then I will declare to them, 'I never knew you; go away from me, you evildoers'."[11] Doing "the will of the Father in heaven" means submission to the will of Allāh, which is the meaning Islām: to submit oneself to His Oneness (*al-istislām lillāhi bil-tawḥīd*) and to obey him through compliance with the law (*al-inqiyād lahū bil-ṭāʿah*) and to disavow the worship of other deities and those who fall into it (*al-barāʾah min al-shirk wa ahlihī*). This is the same message given by Jesus in the above citation. Further, Jesus disavows those who worship him by invoking him and doing deeds in his name and affirms that only those who worship Allāh, obey Him and perform His will shall attain salvation.

In essence, Jesus was a caller to **Islām** and **Tawḥīd**. He neither called to "Judaism" nor to "Christianity". Rather, he called to the way of Abraham and Moses (عَلَيْهِمَاٱلسَّلَامُ).

The true followers of Jesus and his message were led by **James the Just**, and were pure monotheists. They believed in Jesus as a Prophet and Messiah. They observed the law, did not eat pork or drink alcohol and were circumcised. They considered salvation to be through faith *and* deeds which is a central message of the Noble Qurʾān.

This original "Jewish Christianity" was rejected by Jewish leaders out of pride, arrogance and the desire to preserve their standing. It was altered by Paul (Saul of Tarsus) for a Greco-Roman pagan audience. The earliest believers and loyal followers of Jesus were deemed heretical, persecuted and driven out. As a result, "Jewish Christianity" became obscure. Pagan Greco-Roman "Christianity" went on to replace the pure monotheism and law of Jesus (عَلَيْهِٱلسَّلَامُ) through the aid of empire and became the followed religion of many nations and civilisations till this day.

---

[11] Matthew. 7 :21-22.

Argumentation with Jews and Christians

Allāh (عَزَّوَجَلَّ) stated:

وَلَا تُجَٰدِلُوٓاْ أَهْلَ ٱلْكِتَٰبِ إِلَّا بِٱلَّتِى هِىَ أَحْسَنُ إِلَّا ٱلَّذِينَ ظَلَمُواْ مِنْهُمْ وَقُولُوٓاْ ءَامَنَّا بِٱلَّذِىٓ أُنزِلَ إِلَيْنَا وَأُنزِلَ إِلَيْكُمْ وَإِلَٰهُنَا وَإِلَٰهُكُمْ وَٰحِدٌ وَنَحْنُ لَهُۥ مُسْلِمُونَ

"And do not argue with the People of the Scripture except in a way that is best, except for those who commit injustice among them, and say, 'We believe in that which has been revealed to us and revealed to you. And our God and your God is one; and we are Muslims [in submission] to Him'." (29:46).

The Qurʾānic exegete, Imām al-Saʿdī (d. 1956) stated: "The Exalted has prohibited disputing the People of the Scripture when it is done without insight and without any pleasingly acceptable principle. [It orders] that they should only argue in a way that is best: with good manners, gentleness and softness in speech; inviting to the truth; beautifying it; refuting the falsehood and censuring it and using the nearest of ways leading to it. [It explains] that the intent should not be mere argumentation in and of itself, desiring to dominate [others] and for the love of exaltation. Rather, the intent should be to clarify the truth and guide the creation."[12]

Muslims are commanded to engage in dialogue, debate and discussion within certain parameters wherein it is not argument merely for argument's sake but a sincere desire to know and pursue the truth and to guide others to it. It will become clear to any reasonable, fair-minded, objective, intelligent person that what Islām presents on the subject of Jesus (عَلَيْهِ ٱلسَّلَامُ) agrees with authentic scripture, sound reason and an objective analysis of what is left and available of the credible historical record regarding the earliest followers of Jesus.[13]

Allāh (عَزَّوَجَلَّ) also stated:

---

[12] *Taysīr al-Karīm al-Raḥmān* (Beirut: Muʿassasah al-Risālah, 2002) p. 632.

[13] One can refer to the works of scholars such as James Dunn, Bart Ehrman, E.P. Sanders and Robert Eisenman which cover the *historical figure* of Jesus, how Jesus was turned into God and what the Dead Sea scrolls have added to our knowledge of the early sects and followers of Jesus.

قُلْ يَا أَهْلَ الْكِتَابِ تَعَالَوْا إِلَىٰ كَلِمَةٍ سَوَاءٍ بَيْنَنَا وَبَيْنَكُمْ أَلَّا نَعْبُدَ إِلَّا اللَّهَ وَلَا نُشْرِكَ بِهِ شَيْئًا وَلَا يَتَّخِذَ بَعْضُنَا بَعْضًا أَرْبَابًا مِّن دُونِ اللَّهِ فَإِن تَوَلَّوْا فَقُولُوا اشْهَدُوا بِأَنَّا مُسْلِمُونَ

"Say [O Muḥammad]: 'O people of the Scripture [Jews and Christians]: Come to a word that is just between us and you, that we worship none but Allāh, and that we associate no partners with Him, and that none of us shall take others as lords besides Allāh.' Then, if they turn away, say: 'Bear witness that we are Muslims'." (3:64).

Imām al-Saʿdī said: "This means: Let us unite upon this, a word upon which all the Prophets and Messengers were agreed and which was not opposed except by the stubborn and misguided. It is not specific to any one of us but is addressed to all of us and this is from justice in speech and fairness in argument. So let us single out Allāh with worship by singling Him out with our love, fear and hope. Let us not associate a prophet, angel, saint, statue, idol, the animate or inanimate with Him."[14]

This is the basis of dialogue between Muslims and Jews and Christians. The common word of agreement is that we all single out Allāh in worship, exclusive of all other deities devised and invented by men; that we do not erect our priests and rabbis as lords besides Allāh; and that we combine between faith and righteous works through adherence to unadulterated law, only worshipping Allāh through what He legislated and commanded in authentic revealed scripture. This being the way of Abraham, Moses, Jesus (عَلَيْهِمُ السَّلَامُ) and of all the Prophets and Messengers sent by Allāh.

Muḥammad (صَلَّى ٱللَّهُ عَلَيْهِ وَسَلَّمَ) is the last and final messenger and the Qurʾān is the lasting inimitable testimony to the veracity and truthfulness of his prophethood. It clarifies the truth of that wherein the people of previous scripture differed and invites them to reflect and ponder upon these truths and to submit to them—in which case they would be true followers of Abraham, Moses and Jesus (عَلَيْهِمُ السَّلَامُ).

---

[14] *Taysīr al-Karīm al-Raḥmān*, pp. 133-134.

Jesus in Christianity

The earliest "Jewish Christians"[15]—referred to as the Nazarenes and Ebionites—were monotheists, affirmed faith in Jesus as Prophet and Messiah and observed the law, the Torah. They combined between faith and works and held both were necessary for salvation. However, "Nazarene" is best viewed as an umbrella term which consists of a spectrum of "Jewish Christianities". Some sects were closer to the Jewish view of Jesus as Messiah and upholder of the law. They rejected Paul as an imposter and apostate from the law. And others were closer to the Pauline view of Jesus as the "Son of God", but they did not abandon their observance of the law.

The earliest Nazarenes were the Jewish inhabitants of Nazareth who followed Jesus. They were referred to by the Jewish leaders who rejected Jesus as *ha-nozrim*. As for those who exaggerated in Jesus and claimed he was the "Son of God", the Qur'ān refers to them:

وَقَالَتِ ٱلنَّصَٰرَى ٱلْمَسِيحُ ٱبْنُ ٱللَّهِ ذَٰلِكَ قَوْلُهُم بِأَفْوَٰهِهِمْ يُضَٰهِـُٔونَ قَوْلَ ٱلَّذِينَ كَفَرُوا۟ مِن قَبْلُ

"And the Nazarenes (Christians) say: Jesus is the Son of Allāh. That is their statement from their mouths; they imitate the statement of those who disbelieved [before them]" (9:30).

Historians and academics have pointed out the existence of these "Jewish Christianities" on the basis of research of available sources.

As for those closer to the "Purely Jewish" wing:

"Jewish followers of Jesus included the Nazarenes, or Nazoreans, and the Ebionites (from the Hebrew *ebyonim*, the poor). In their writings, they proclaimed faith in Jesus as the last prophet and as the Messiah of the Israel who had not come to abolish the Law of Moses (Matt. 5:17) but to purify it from false interpretations. They emphasized that Jesus followed the model set by the Prophet

[15] "Christ" is the Latinized Greek translation of the Hebrew "mashiach". It is inaccurate to refer to the original followers of Jesus as "Christians". We employ the term "Jewish Christians" to distinguish them from the Israelite faction who rejected Jesus and the Pauline faction who deified him.

Jeremiah who denounced 'the false pen of the scribes' (Jer. 8:8) and attacked spurious laws regarding animal sacrifices (Jer. 7:21-26)."[16]

And also: "The Ebionite Christians... believed that Jesus was the Jewish Messiah sent from the Jewish God to the Jewish people in fulfilment of the Jewish Scriptures. They also believed that to belong to the people of God, one needed to be Jewish. As a result, they insisted on observing the Sabbath, keeping kosher, and circumcising all males... An early source, Irenaeus, also reports that the Ebionites continued reverence to Jerusalem, evidently by praying in its direction during their daily acts of worship."[17]

And as for those closer to the "Pauline Jewish" wing:

"The evidence provided by the Church Fathers appear to demonstrate that the Nazarenes, a Jewish Christian group orthodox in all respects except for their practice of the ceremonial law, existed as a distinct group from the time of the fall of Jerusalem until the late fourth or early fifth century. They were descendants of the Jewish Christian church in Jerusalem, which escaped to Pella after the fall of Jerusalem. They recognized the authority of the Apostle Paul and his mission to the Gentiles, as well as the authority of the greater Church, of which they considered themselves apart. They evangelized their Jewish brethren in the synagogues. They accepted the entirety of the Scriptures, both the Old and New Testaments. They acknowledged that God was the Creator of all things and that Jesus Christ was the Son of God."[18]

References to "Jewish Christianity" are made by numerous early Church authorities.[19] Justin Martyr (d. 165) spoke of some Jews "who admit that he is Christ, while holding him to be man of men."[20]

Iraneus (d. 202), the Bishop of Lyon, wrote of the Ebionites in his work, *Against Heresies*, stating: "They... repudiate the Apostle Paul,

---

[16] Jongeneel, J. *Jesus Christ in World History: His Presence and Representation in Cyclical and Linear Settings*. Peter Lang GmbH (2009) p. 85.

[17] Bart Ehrman in *Lost Christianities* (2003) p. 99-102.

[18] Kenneth Howard (1993). *Jewish Christianity in the Early Church*. p. 33.

[19] The citations that follow from the five authorities have been taken from Akyol, M. *The Islāmic Jesus*. St. Martin's Press (2017), Chapter II: The Jewish Christian "Heresy".

[20] In *Dialogue with Trypho*, Chapter XLVIII, available online.

maintaining that he was an apostate from the law. As to the prophetical writings, they endeavour to expound them in a somewhat singular manner: they practice circumcision, persevere in the observance of those customs which are enjoined by the law, and are so Judaic in their style of life, that they even adore Jerusalem as if it were the house of God."[21]

Eusebius (d. 339) made mention of the Ebionites as a heretical sect, noting their "deviation" that Christ was "a common and plain man, who was justified only because of his superior virtue." He went on to explain that some of the Ebionites accepted the virgin birth, "but refuse to acknowledge that he pre-existed, being God, Word and Wisdom." Eusebius also mentioned that they reject all the epistles of the apostle (meaning Paul) whom they deemed "an apostate from the law". He also said that they only use the Gospel of the Hebrews which is lost. It exists only as brief citations in the works of church fathers which also indicate the existence of a Gospel of the Ebionites and a Gospel of the Nazarenes.[22]

Epiphanius (d. 403), Bishop of the city of Salamis, Cyprus also made mention of Ebionites and Nazarenes whom he considered as poisonous snakes whose venom represented heresies. In his book called "Medicine" he mentions that they follow a Gospel of the Hebrews, despise Paul, denied the divinity of Jesus, and saw him only as a "true prophet". He said of them, "They are Jews and nothing else" but noted that even the Jews maligned them three times a day in their synagogues, invoking, "May God curse the Nazoreans."[23]

Jerome (d. 420), a priest and theologian, wrote about Jewish Christians he met in Antioch (northern coast of Syria). He described them as Nazarenes "who accept Christ in such a way that they do not cease to observe the old Law". He mentioned that they used a Gospel of the Hebrews written originally in Aramaic with Hebrew letters, later translated into Greek. In this lost gospel, Jerome reports that

---

[21] In *Against Heresies*, Volume 1 Chapter 26, available online.

[22] In his *Church History: Life of Constantine*, The Heresy of the Ebionites (Ch. 27), available online.

[23] In *Panarion*, 29.9.1 and 29.9.2 quoted in Broadhead, K. *Jewish Ways of Following Jesus*. Mohr Siebeck (2010), p. 176.

James the Just was the most prominent disciple of Jesus. Jerome also noted that this "Jewish-Christian heresy" is found in all parts of the East where the Jews have their synagogues.[24]

The original Jewish Christianity led by James was rejected by the Jewish elders on the one hand, and on the other, it was neglected by the canonical gospel writers and overshadowed by the Pauline Greco-Roman development of Christianity. This lead to the complete loss of its monotheistic character and the essentiality of observance of law to the actualisation of faith. This also made it easier to win converts through a nominal form of Christianity for pagan audiences without the burdens of observance of law.

The Christians then differed and disputed as they argued about the nature of Jesus and the divine essence as noted in the Qurʾān:

فَٱخْتَلَفَ ٱلْأَحْزَابُ مِنۢ بَيْنِهِمْ

"**Then the factions differed [concerning Jesus] from among themselves.**" (19:37).

As for Paulinism, after persecuting the followers of Jesus—those who had actually met him, heard him, believed in him, and learned from him directly—Paul [Saul] of Tarsus (d. 67), who had never met Jesus and cites almost nothing from Jesus in his writings, recast the Jewish Messiah of the Children of Israel, into a deified Lord.

Paul styled himself an apostle "among the Gentiles" and preached a Jesus doctrine that Greek Gentiles could believe in: a deified saviour, a redeemer of sins, in whom a personalized faith could be held without observance of law. Likewise, Paul taught a bodily resurrection that resembles the deities of the mystery cults such as Isis, Attis and Mithra. Finally, Paul ascribed divinity to Jesus by conferring divine attributes to him, turning him into an "incarnate son". This would not be far removed from the then prevailing beliefs of the Greeks in Zeus and Apollo.

"Paul's interpretation of the Christ figure bears the unmistakable stamp of a saviour figure of the Greek mystery religions into whose form Jesus was cast. The statements of Jesus Himself, however, do

---

[24] Refer to Broadhead, K. *Jewish Ways of Following Jesus*. Mohr Siebeck (2010), pp. 164-174.

not support His exaltation to the Godhead... With the gradual demise of the Jewish wing of Christianity Paul's Christology came to the forefront in the Christian understanding on Jesus. His glorification of Christ's divinity has played a major role in the deification of Jesus."[25]

"Towards the end of the 1st century, and during the 2nd, many learned men came over both from Judaism and paganism to Christianity. These brought with them into the Christian schools of theology their Platonic ideas and phraseology."[26] "The use of Greek philosophy in Christian theology had far-reaching consequences for the core of Christology: the ontological terms *ousia*, *physis* and *prosopon* were introduced to explain and safeguard the mystery of Jesus Christ. In the process the Christian faith was dejudaized and Hellenized."[27]

In Roman (Constantine) Christianity, Jesus became the "Sun-God"[28] and under the influence of Greek philosophy and its discussions of substance, soul, mind, spirit, as well as influence from pagan myths,[29] the Trinity received its complete formulation after considerable debate had taken place regarding Jesus and the nature of the divine over a couple of centuries.[30]

---

[25] Jack Mclean in *The Deification of Jesus*. World Order, Spring Summer edition, 1980, p. 24.

[26] Mclintock, J. and Strong, J. in *Cyclopaedia of Biblical, Theological, and Ecclesiastical Literature*, 1891, Vol. 10, "Trinity," p. 553).

[27] Jongeneel, J. *Jesus Christ in World History.* (2009) p. 91.

[28] See *Jesus Christ, Sun of God: Ancient Cosmology and Early Christian Symbolism by* David Fideler, Quest Books (1993). Historian Henry Chadwick writes, "Constantine, like his father, worshipped the Unconquered Sun... His conversion should not be interpreted as an inward experience of grace... It was a military matter." *The Early Church*, (1993) pp. 122-125.

[29] Marie Sinclair, Countess of Caithness, in her 1876 book, states: "It is generally, although erroneously, supposed that the doctrine of the Trinity is of Christian origin. Nearly every nation of antiquity possessed a similar doctrine. St. Jerome testifies unequivocally, 'All the ancient nations believed in the Trinity'." *Old Truths in a New Light*. p. 381.

[30] "The Nicene and Constantine creeds (325 and 381) confessed Jesus as being 'of the same substance' (*homoousios*) as God the Father. But they failed to put an end to the bitter Christological disputes that divided the early church... the fourth Ecumenical council of Chalcedon (451) produced a new

"Through a series of creeds based on theological speculation Jesus the Son was declared to be the very essence of Divinity walking upon the earth, the Godhead itself united with a deified Holy Spirit in a Trinitarian theology. These creeds, far from descending upon the church fathers as divine revelation, underwent a long historical development that was not uncontested. They were finally elaborated in their present form after four centuries of acrimonious theological quarrelling that necessitated four world councils of the church—those of Nicea, Ephesus, Constantinople, and Chalcedon—that brought in their wake bloody warfare among Christian factions. These Christological controversies resulted in the fragmentation of the churches of Asia Minor from those of Greek Orthodox Constantinople, a fragmentation that has continued to this day."[31]

Concepts of *trinity*, *begotten son*, *sun-god*, *resurrection*, *rebirth* and *redemption* were widespread during that era with respect to the deities of the Egyptians, Greeks, Persians, and Romans such as Osiris, Horus, Isis, Mithra, Dionysus, Attis and Bāl. Within this climate of ideas and mystery religions, Jesus was deified and worshipped. It became more or less impossible for any 'Christian' to know and practice the true way of Jesus less than a few centuries after him, the original "Jewish Christianity" having becoming obscure.

As Christianity spread across the Mediterranean and European lands, local pagan symbols (such as the cross for example), customs, traditions, and festivals (such as the solstices and equinoxes for example)[32] were co-opted by the Church to win converts because rural pagan populations were unwilling to let go of these practices. In reality, it was not that pagans adopted Christianity, but more that Christianity adopted paganism. "The reign of Constantine marks the epoch of the transformation of Christianity from a religion into a

---

language hoping to solve the Christological problem once and for all..." Jongeneel, J. *Jesus Christ in World History.* (2009) p. 90.

[31] MacLean, J. *The Deification of Jesus.* World Order, Spring/Summer edition, 1980, p. 23.

[32] "Not only were Pagan festival days changed into Christian holydays, but Pagan idols were converted into Christian saints, and Pagan temples into Christian churches." Doane, T. W. *Bible Myths and Their Parallels in Other Religions.* New York: The Commonwealth Company. 1882. p. 396.

political system; and though, in one sense, that system was degraded into an idolatry, in another it had risen into a development of the old Greek mythology. The maxim holds good in the social as well as in the mechanical world, that, when two bodies strike, the form of both is changed. Paganism was modified by Christianity; Christianity by Paganism"[33]

"The early Christian saints, bishops, and fathers, confessedly adopted the liturgies, rites, ceremonies, and terms of heathenism; making it their boast, that the pagan religion, properly explained, really was nothing else than Christianity; that the best and wisest of its professors, in all ages, had been Christians all along; that Christianity was but a name more recently acquired to a religion which had previously existed, and had been known to the Greek philosophers... That Christianity is nothing more than Paganism under a new name, has, as we said above, been admitted over and over again by the Fathers of the Church, and others. Aringhus (in his account of subterraneous Rome) acknowledges the conformity between the Pagan and Christian form of worship, and defends the admission of the ceremonies of heathenism into the service of the Church, by the authority of the wisest prelates and governors, whom, lie says, found it necessary, in the conversion of the Gentiles, to dissemble, and wink at many things, and yield to the times; and not to use force against customs which the people were so obstinately fond of... We have seen, then, that the only difference between Christianity and Paganism is that Brahma, Ormuzd, Osiris, Zeus, Jupiter, etc., are called by another name; Crishna, Buddha, Bacchus, Adonis, Mithras, etc., have been turned into Christ Jesus: Venus pigeon into the Holy Ghost ; Diana, Isis, Devaki, etc., into the Virgin Mary; and the demi-gods and heroes into saints. The exploits of the one were represented as the miracles of the other. Pagan festivals became Christian holidays, and Pagan temples became Christian churches."[34]

---

[33] John William Draper in *History of the Conflict Between Religion and Science*. New York: Appleton and Company. 1875. pp. 50-52.

[34] Doane, T. W. *Bible Myths*, p. 407-413.

From the above we can summarise the various stages of what eventually became known as "Christianity":

First: Jesus as Prophet and Messiah was followed by believers from the Children of Israel who observed the law. The multitudes of believers in this time led by the apostle James only knew him as a prophet. They believed that salvation was through faith and deeds. **Second:** Paul (Saul of Tarsus) then cast Jesus as an incarnated divine figure and personal saviour cloaked with mystery-religion language that was familiar to the Greeks. Paul did away with the law. This was "Paulinism", a big departure from "Jewish Christianity" and was a new, innovated rendition of the figure and mission of Jesus. It was rejected and opposed by faithful adherents of the teachings of Jesus, the "Jewish Christians". **Third:** Evangelists and storytellers weaved the Pauline version of *belief about Jesus* into their writings of the gospels, whilst neglecting and sidelining the actual *beliefs of Jesus* as preserved in the true Gospel with the movement of James. Paulinism later became "official Christianity" through the aid of empire whilst the original "Jewish Christianity" faded away into obscurity. **Fourth:** The adoption of Greek philosophical and mystery-religion concepts within Roman Christianity, leading to the formulation of the Trinity. **Fifth:** The absorption of other local pagan ideas, customs, rites and rituals during the Church's use of political power to spread Pauline Greco-Roman Christianity across the Mediterranean and Europe, thereby enhancing its pagan form, flavour and character.

Today, the three primary Christian divisions are:

a) the **Roman Catholic** division,

b) the **Protestant** division which broke off from Catholicism in the 16th century and these two are referred to as the "Western Church" and,

c) the **Orthodox** division of the "Eastern Church".

All of these divisions believe in the Trinity and in the divinity of Jesus, that as the Son "Jesus is consubstantial [of the same substance and essence] with the Father" meaning that "the Son is one and the same God" and that he is "one in substance and triune in three persons". This, in the teachings and messages of all of the Prophets, including Jesus himself, is **associationism** (*shirk*) [to associate partners with God in divinity and worship] and contradicts pure monotheistic belief as well as sound reason and common sense.

As for the Protestants, they reject the absolute authority of the Catholic Pope and the belief in his infallibility. They also reject many beliefs and traditions of Catholicism absorbed from Pagan culture after the time of Constantine. They split into many sects differing with each other as to what degree they accept and reject such beliefs and traditions. Protestants claim to have "purified the Biblical faith" by rejecting veneration of Mary, the worship of saints and the rituals, ceremonies and traditions absorbed from Paganism. However, they still believe in Pauline heresies regarding the divinity of Jesus as well as the Trinity, both of which are unsupported by authentic, uncorrupted revelation.

Today, many Christians—the majority of them being women—are converting to Islām because of three main reasons:

a) the overwhelming historical proof that what became known as "Christianity" after Jesus until today is not the religion that Jesus believed, practised and called to. Rather, that it was a later development through accretion and syncretisation[35] and,

b) disillusionment with its confusing, contradictory theology that a critical mind is unable to decipher. Mystery does not offer satisfactory answers about divinity and many of these women converts state that they find a clear and intelligible treatment of divinity in Islām.[36]

---

[35] In other words, the attempts to harmonise and unify the gradually accumulated novel concepts and doctrines pertaining to Jesus and his nature over the first few centuries after Jesus.

[36] Refer to "*Women and Conversion to Islām: The American Women's Experience*" by Elkoubaiti Naoualv, 2010. News headlines over the past twenty years abound in this regard: "*Fast-growing Islām Winning Converts in the Western World*", CNN, 14 April 1997. "*Why are so Many Modern British Career Women Converting to Islām*", Daily Mail, 28 October 2010. "*Europeans Increasingly Converting to Islam*", Gatestone Institute, 27 January 2012. "*Converting to Islām: British Women on Prayer, peace and Prejudice*", Guardian UK, 11 October 2013. "*Rise of Islāmic Converts Challenges France*", NY Times, 2 February 2013. "*Converts to Islām increase after French attack*", World Bulletin, 24 February 2015. "*More in France are Turning to Islām, Challenging a Nation's Idea of Itself*", NY Times, 3 February 2013. "*Islām is Ireland's Fastest Growing*

c) the absence of clear guidance in affairs of worship, personal and social dealings and other areas of life, leading to confusing, hazy notions of morality and the absence of moral certitude. Jesus came to affirm the law, not to abolish it, as was done in Pauline Greco-Roman Christianity. Islām provides comprehensive guidance in all of these matters, providing clear direction.

Serious modern scholarship with respect to Jesus, his message and his early followers is now establishing a pictorial framework that increasingly resembles the portrayal of Jesus in the Qur'ān and Prophetic traditions: A Prophet who was not divine, never claimed to be and was followed by Israelites upholding and observing the law. His earliest loyal followers, led by James the Just, believed in him as a Prophet and never understood him to be divine.[37] He was given miracles to establish the veracity of his prophethood to the Children of Israel. In contrast, Paul, who never even met Jesus, developed Greco-Roman pagan mystery-religion doctrines in opposition to the beliefs and practices of the true, loyal and direct followers of Jesus.

In Matthew's Gospel we are informed of the following (emphasis added): "When the chief priests and Pharisees heard the parables of Jesus, they knew he was speaking about them. Although they wanted to arrest him, *they feared the crowds, because they considered Jesus a prophet.*"[38] This provides evidence that the followers of Jesus were monotheists who worshipped Allāh alone and believed Jesus to be a Prophet, a Messiah and nothing more.

His deification took place afterwards and was written into the gospels through the writings of evangelists and storytellers. When

---

Religion", International Business Times, 21 February 2014. This article points out that most of the converts are women. "*Lifting the Veil on Ireland's Fastest Growing Religion*", Independent Ireland, 21 September 2014. "*Islām Growing in America*", US Department of Defence, 4 October 2001. "*Hispanic Islāmic Converts Find Comfort in God and Latino Culture*", Huffington Post, 11 September 2012.

[37] For further research one can study: Ehrman, B. D. *How Jesus Became God*. HarperCollins, 2014; Eisenman, Robert. *The Dead Sea Scrolls and the Roots of Christianity and Islam*. Grave Distractions Publications; 2nd edition (2014); Sanders, E. P. *The Historical Figure of Jesus*. Allen Lane: 1st edition (1993).

[38] Matthew 21:45-56.

the actual statements of Jesus are extracted and analysed, no Pauline doctrines are found therein or can be justified through them. These gospels were written *after* the writing of Paul's epistles. The anonymous pro-Pauline storytellers weaved these doctrines into their writing of the gospels, and imposed their views *about* Jesus onto the gospels.

The Christians are cautioned by their Lord and Creator, Allāh—the Lord of Moses and Jesus—and are informed of the enormity of what they have fallen into:

لَقَدْ كَفَرَ الَّذِينَ قَالُوا إِنَّ اللَّهَ هُوَ الْمَسِيحُ ابْنُ مَرْيَمَ وَقَالَ الْمَسِيحُ يَا بَنِي إِسْرَائِيلَ اعْبُدُوا اللَّهَ رَبِّي وَرَبَّكُمْ إِنَّهُ مَن يُشْرِكْ بِاللَّهِ فَقَدْ حَرَّمَ اللَّهُ عَلَيْهِ الْجَنَّةَ وَمَأْوَاهُ النَّارُ وَمَا لِلظَّالِمِينَ مِنْ أَنصَارٍ

"They have certainly disbelieved who say, 'Allāh is the Messiah, the son of Mary' whereas the Messiah [actually] said, 'O Children of Israel, worship Allāh, my Lord and your Lord.' Indeed, he who associates others with Allāh, Allāh has forbidden him Paradise, and his refuge is the Fire. And there are not for the wrongdoers any helpers." (5:72).

However, noticeable traces of truth still exist within the gospel.

From them is the statement in Mark 12:29: "'The most important one,' answered Jesus, 'is this: '*Hear, O Israel: The Lord our God, the Lord is one*'." Meaning, He who alone deserves to be worshipped is one. The words *eloh* (אֱלֹהַּ), *ilāh* (إله) are identical in Hebrew, Aramaic and Arabic and this statement of Jesus rejects worship for **anything and everything** besides Allāh.

The words *eloh* and *ilāh* refer to anything to which worship and devotion is given for the fulfilment of needs that can only be met independently by the Creator alone. Thus deities can be very many and this statement of Jesus rejects their worship and renders it false and in vain. The statement *lā ilāha illallāh*, part of the declaration of Islām, is identical to the declaration of Jesus and of all previous Prophets and Messengers.

Jesus in Talmudic [Rabbinic] Judaism

As has preceded, Jesus (عَلَيْهِ السَّلَام) was sent to revive the religion of Islām brought by Moses— *tawḥīd*, pure monotheism, in belief *and* practice—and to purify and confirm his law which had been altered. Also, to clarify the differing which the Children of Israel had fallen into amongst themselves pertaining to matters of belief and law. The Jews—under the influence of nations such as Egypt, Babylon and Persia—had been affected by paganism, idolatry, magic and astrology and had also distorted much of the Torah by their own inventions and interpolations.

The Pharisees who were the elitist religious elders[39] of the time asserted another divine law, the "oral tradition"—later put in writing as the Talmud—which they had used to abrogate and distort the Mosaic law in the name of explanation and legal interpretation,

---

[39] The "religious elders" who resided in Babylon from the 6th century BC onwards authored a new doctrine based upon race, nationality and land after a history of conflict and battle over land. This was the foundation of a new religion called "Judaism"—a departure from the "Islām" of Moses— and was no longer centred around calling nations to monotheism, but around race, nationalism and land and protection of the "national identity". They weaved it into their authorship of the Torah and also claimed a revealed "oral tradition" had been passed on through initiation since the time of Moses. This later became the Mishnah and its commentary, the Gemara, as the Talmud in written form (after the era of Jesus). Despite claims of adherence to monotheism, this oral tradition was a mixture of the dictates of religious leaders, occultism, gnostic-spirituality, magic (matters they had picked up from other nations such as the Egyptians, Babylonians and Persians) and the shackles of invented observances, statutes and laws that became the basis for a despotic micro-management by religious leaders of the lives of ordinary Jews. It superseded the original Torah given to Moses, though it is claimed to be an elaboration of it. The religious leaders assumed divine authority and demanded absolute obedience, even in their distortion of scripture. This religion is known as "Rabbinic Judaism" (God continuing to speak to the Jewish nation through the Rabbis, the religious scholarly elite, who possess a divine character) and has remained the dominant form of religion practiced by most Jews till today. Thus, the religion of Islām of Moses (and of all Prophets) and the task of preaching monotheism to the world that was left with the Children of Israel was turned by the religious elite into a racial, tribal, nationalistic doctrine centred around land.

thereby assuming divine authority for themselves. Jesus's opposition to their doctrine and his severe repudiation of their ancestors' past deeds and their "traditions of the elders" brought him scorn.

Jesus (عَلَيْهِ ٱلسَّلَامُ) is reported in the Gospels to have said: "Woe to you, scribes and Pharisees, you hypocrites! You build tombs for the prophets and decorate the monuments of the righteous. And you say, 'If we had lived in the days of our fathers, we would not have been partners with them in shedding the blood of the prophets.' So you testify against yourselves that you are the sons of those who murdered the prophets."[40] As for the mention of tombs and monuments, this is similar to what eventually entered the Muslim nation—as prophesied by Muḥammad (صَلَّى ٱللَّٰهُ عَلَيْهِ وَسَلَّمَ)—among the grave-worshippers who build mausoleums and tombs and offer worship to the inhabitants who are claimed to provide intercession, fulfilment of needs and removal of calamities. It is what Muḥammad (صَلَّى ٱللَّٰهُ عَلَيْهِ وَسَلَّمَ) warned against, cursing those [from the Jews and Christians] who had taken the graves of their Prophets as places of worship, an act that lead them ultimately to worship the Prophets themselves. This was a warning to the Muslim nation, lest they follow in the same footsteps.[41]

According to the Gospels:

"And the Pharisees and the scribes asked him [Jesus], 'Why do your disciples not walk according to the traditions of the elders?'" Jesus replied: "You have disregarded the commandment of God to keep the tradition of men." He went on to say, "You neatly set aside the commandment of God to maintain your own tradition... Thus you make the word of God of none effect by your tradition that you have handed down."[42] It is also related that Jesus said: "You hypocrites!

---

[40] Matthew 23:29-31.

[41] In the ḥadīth of ʿĀʾishah (رَضِيَ ٱللَّٰهُ عَنْهَا) who said that the Messenger (صَلَّى ٱللَّٰهُ عَلَيْهِ وَسَلَّمَ) said: "*May Allāh curse the Jews and Christians, they took the graves of the Prophets as places of worship.*" Related by al-Bukhārī and Muslim. Despite these severe warnings, Muslim sects since around the 4th-5th centuries hijrah (11th-12th centuries CE) have followed in their footsteps—as the Messenger also prophesied—and fallen into worship of saints and tombs.

[42] Mark 7:5-9. The "traditions of the elders" were not in written form at the time of Jesus, but were later committed to writing as the Babylonian

Isaiah prophesied correctly about you: 'These people honour Me [God] with their lips, but their hearts are far from Me. They worship Me in vain; they teach as doctrine the precepts of men.'"[43]

The issues raised by Jesus were a) pure monotheism (*tawḥīd*), since some amongst the Jews had fallen into **associationism** (*shirk*) and other grave sins and b) following the law faithfully (*ittibāʾ*), since the Jewish religious elders had disobeyed the law and innovated their own doctrines. They also distorted the law through clever semantic devices, additions and alterations. Plots were hatched against Jesus. He faced accusations of idolatry and of performing miracles through magic. He was subsequently depicted in Talmudic literature as a madman, idolater and sorcerer[44] and his mother, Mary (عَلَيْهَاالسَّلَام) was reviled and accused of enormous things.[45] The early Jewish believers in Jesus were branded as heretics and referred to as *ha-nozrim*, followers of *yeshu ha-nozri* (Jesus of Nazareth). They were considered more dangerous than Jesus himself because of their threat to the "national existence".[46]

With the development of the Pauline Greco-Roman rendition of Jesus, Jews countered the exaggerated status of Jesus in the Gospels by providing a counter-narrative in the Babylonian Talmud. Studies in this contested subject have convincingly established the existence

---

Talmud, consisting of two parts: a) the Mishnah, which is the basic oral law that was the subject of contention between Jesus and Pharisees which was put into writing around 200 years after Jesus and b) the Gemara which is the commentary upon the Mishnah and is the essence of the Talmud.

[43] Matthew 15:7-9.

[44] Refer to "*Jesus Christ in the Talmud, Midrash, Zohar and the Liturgy of the Synagogue: Texts and Translations*" by Dr. Gustaf Dalman, translated into English by A.W. Streane, Deighton Bell, Cambridge, 1893, and the more academic work by the expert, prolific scholar and Professor of Jewish Studies, Peter Schäfer, "*Jesus in the Talmud*", Princeton University Press, 2009.

[45] In Sanhedrin 106a, she is accused of "playing the harlot with carpenters." *The Babylonian Talmud*, The Soncino Press, London, (1936). The editors note, "Though no name is mentioned to shew which woman is meant, the mother of Jesus may be alluded to, which theory is strengthened by the statement that she mated with a carpenter."

[46] Refer to Jongeneel, J. *Jesus Christ in World History.* (2009) p. 83.

of a highly repugnant, vilifying Talmudic image of Jesus (عَلَيْهِ السَّلَام) and numerous studies exist in this regard.

In his book "*Jesus in the Talmud*", Professor of Jewish Studies at Princeton University Peter Schafer writes—on the basis of his studies of manuscripts—that the various pieces in the Talmud (often with cryptic references) present, "polemical counter-narratives that parody the New Testament stories, most notably the story of Jesus' birth and death. They ridicule Jesus' birth from a virgin, as maintained by the Gospels of Matthew and Luke, and they contest fervently the claim that Jesus is the Messiah and the Son of God. Most remarkably, they counter the New Testament Passion story with its message of the Jews' guilt and shame as Christ killers. Instead, they reverse it completely: yes, they maintain, we accept responsibility for it, but there is no reason to feel ashamed because we rightfully executed a blasphemer and idolater. Jesus deserved death, and he got what he deserved. Accordingly, they subvert the Christian idea of Jesus' resurrection by having him punished forever in hell and by making clear that this fate awaits his followers as well, who believe in this impostor."[47]

Professor Israel Shahak writes: "It must be admitted at the outset that the Talmud and the Talmudic literature... contains very offensive statements and precepts directed specifically against Christianity. For example, in addition to a series of scurrilous sexual allegations against Jesus, the Talmud states that his punishment in hell is to be immersed in boiling excrement—a statement not exactly calculated to endear the Talmud to devout Christians. Or one can quote the precept according to which Jews are instructed to burn, publicly if possible, any copy of the New Testament that comes into their hands."[48]

On a Chabad[49] sponsored website, the following is stated: "The Talmud (Babylonian edition) records other sins of 'Jesus the

---

[47] *Jesus in the Talmud*. Princeton University Press, (2007) p. 9.

[48] Professor Israel Shahak such as "*Jewish History, Jewish Religion*" London: Pluto (2002) p. 25.

[49] Chabad is an Orthodox Jewish movement based around mysticism, [similar to the Ṣūfīs and their doctrine of the Unity of Existence (waḥdat al-

Nazarene': 1. He and his disciples practiced sorcery and black magic, led Jews astray into idolatry, and were sponsored by foreign, gentile powers for the purpose of subverting Jewish worship (Sanhedrin 43a). 2. He was sexually immoral, worshipped statues of stone (a brick is mentioned), was cut off from the Jewish people for his wickedness, and refused to repent (Sanhedrin 107b; Sotah 47a). 3. He learned witchcraft in Egypt and, to perform miracles, used procedures that involved cutting his flesh—which is also explicitly banned in the Bible (Shabbos 104b). The false, rebellious message of Jesus has been thoroughly rejected by the vast majority of the Jewish people, as G-d commanded. Unfortunately, however, this same message has brought a terrible darkness upon the world; today, over 1.5 billion gentiles believe in Jesus. These lost souls mistakenly think they have found salvation in Jesus; tragically, they are in for a rude awakening."[50]

The 1906 Jewish Encyclopedia states, "The Jewish legends in regard to Jesus are found in three sources, each independent of the others—(1) in New Testament apocrypha and Christian polemical works, (2) in the Talmud and the Midrash, and (3) in the life of Jesus ('Toledot Yeshu') that originated in the Middle Ages. It is the tendency of all these sources to belittle the person of Jesus by ascribing to him illegitimate birth, magic, and a shameful death... The earliest authenticated passage ascribing illegitimate birth to Jesus is that in Yeb. iv. 3.... and here occur also the two expressions so often applied to Jesus in later literature—איש פלוני (= 'that anonymous one,' the name of Jesus being avoided) and ממזר (='bastard'; for which in later times איש אותו was used)."[51] For the charges of worshipping Balaam, questioning religious authority and leading Israel astray Jesus is said to be punished in Hellfire in "boiling hot excrement".[52]

wujūd)]. They rely and draw heavily upon the Kabbalah, a system of magic disguised as spirituality.

[50] Refer to http://www.noahide.com/yeshu.htm (accessed 31/3/2017).

[51] The Jewish Encylopedia, Volume 7, p. 170.

[52] Gittin 57a, Gittin, *The Babylonian Talmud*, Volume 21, The Soncino Press, London, (1936), p. 261.

In the Soncino Press translation of the Babylonian Talmud, various footnotes by the editors make clear that the figure of Jesus is being alluded to. The Jewish Encyclopedia also affirms in its entry for "Balaam" that this is a code word for Jesus in Sanhedrin 106b and Gittin 57a.[53] Numerous interviews can be found on Youtube in which Rabbis are questioned about these beliefs and they respond with either candid affirmation,[54] justification (stating "maybe he deserved to die") or evasion.

References to Jesus were obscured by cryptic terms and later medieval versions of the Talmud (and other writings) were edited to avoid reprisals from Christians in Europe.

The unjust and unfounded Talmudic characterisation of Jesus can be summarised in the following points:

- Jesus was guilty of falsehood and heresy
- He was born an illegitimate child of an immoral woman
- He was foolish and insane
- He was a conjurer and a magician
- He was an idolater
- He was a seducer
- He was killed and crucified for his crimes
- He is in Hell immersed in boiling excrement

It should be noted that there are two broad aspects to the Jewish treatment of Jesus and his followers, both the earlier followers and the later ones:

The first is their rejection of Jesus, the Messiah, their resentment of his challenge to their authority, their excommunication of the early Jewish Christians, considering them a threat to the "national existence", to their Jewish identity, and to the religious system they had devised and maintained which protected their interests.

The second is their strong reaction to the deification of Jesus in Pauline Greco-Roman Christianity, considering this to be idolatry

---

[53] The Jewish Encylopedia, Volume 2, p. 469.

[54] For example, Rabbi Felix Rogan, Director of Temple Mount Centre, Jerusalem, states that "our sources" [referring to the Talmud] indicate that "Jesus was a witch or a sorcerer with an eye for the ladies." Refer to the following clip: https://www.youtube.com/watch?v=ouLodOujbbg

and paganism. Since they had already disbelieved in Jesus, they took the opportunity to blame these evils upon him. They used the polytheism and idolatry which appeared afterwards as "Christianity" to justify their continued rejection and vilification of Jesus. Yet Jesus is wholly innocent of this deification and worship and will exonerate himself from it. At the same time, the Jews remain in manifest error for rejecting him out of pride and arrogance.

In explanation of what took place, Allāh (عَزَّوَجَلَّ) stated:

يَٰٓأَيُّهَا ٱلَّذِينَ ءَامَنُوا۟ كُونُوٓا۟ أَنصَارَ ٱللَّهِ كَمَا قَالَ عِيسَى ٱبْنُ مَرْيَمَ لِلْحَوَارِيِّـۧنَ مَنْ أَنصَارِىٓ إِلَى ٱللَّهِ قَالَ ٱلْحَوَارِيُّونَ نَحْنُ أَنصَارُ ٱللَّهِ فَـَٔامَنَت طَّآئِفَةٌ مِّنۢ بَنِىٓ إِسْرَٰٓءِيلَ وَكَفَرَت طَّآئِفَةٌ فَأَيَّدْنَا ٱلَّذِينَ ءَامَنُوا۟ عَلَىٰ عَدُوِّهِمْ فَأَصْبَحُوا۟ ظَٰهِرِينَ

"O you who have believed, be supporters of Allāh, as when Jesus, the Son of Mary, said to the disciples, 'Who are my supporters for Allāh?' The disciples said, 'We are supporters of Allāh.' And a faction of the Children of Israel believed and a faction disbelieved. So We supported [the proof of] those who believed against their enemy, and they became dominant." (61:14).

A group from the Children of Israel rejected Jesus and a group believed, the "Jewish Christians" who are the supporters of Jesus the Messiah. These followers later split into groups and differed with each other. A group remained true believers, upon monotheism and the law, they said that Jesus was the slave and prophet of Allāh who was raised up to Heaven. Others exaggerated in Jesus: Some said he was the Son of Allāh, raised by Allāh to Himself and others said he was Allāh incarnate and rose to the heaven.[55] From here, the path was laid out for further deification and the disappearance of the original message of Jesus.

---

[55] Refer to the Qur'ān commentaries of al-Ṭabarī, Ibn Kathīr, al-Baghawī and others. Al-Ṭabarī explains, citing from Ibn ʿAbbās: That [prior to Islām] the Jacobites said Jesus was Allāh and the Nestorians said Jesus was the son of Allāh, and those who remained Muslims (true monotheists observing the law) said Jesus was the slave and messenger of Allāh. These two factions persecuted the believing faction—the true message of Jesus being obscured thereby—until Muḥammad (صَلَّىٱللَّهُعَلَيْهِوَسَلَّمَ) was sent whereupon the truth became manifest.

Those mentioned in the verse who were supported and became dominant were the Muslims and those Christians who accepted Islām after the coming of Muḥammad (صَلَّى ٱللَّٰهُ عَلَيْهِ وَسَلَّمَ). They were aided by the proof of the Qur᾿ān which established the truth regarding Jesus the Messiah and his mother Mary[56] and they were also victorious over Jews and Christians, when Islām became dominant. The proof of any "Christian" who accepts Islām and the Islāmic viewpoint of Jesus and his mother Mary is dominant over those Christians who have strayed from the true message of Jesus, just as it is dominant over those who rejected and reviled him.

In debates between Muslims and Christians on the subject of the nature of Jesus, the strength of argument of Muslims is clear, apparent, agreeable to instinct, natural disposition, common sense and reason and is supported by a correct reading of the available historical record and authentic revelation, the Qur᾿ān. It is for this reason that large numbers of Western, well-educated though disillusioned Christians are accepting Islām after learning and studying the Qur᾿ānic presentation of Jesus and his message.

The overwhelming reason given by them for their conversion and accepting the Qur᾿ānic account of Jesus is the resolution of conflict and confusion created by incoherent Christian doctrine that had been troubling them, primarily, the Trinity, whose true roots lie in pagan mystery religions.[57] They also come to realise that Muslims are in fact the true followers of Jesus the Messiah.

---

[56] This is the explanation of the early Qur᾿ānic commentators

[57] All of the mental gymnastics used by zealous Christians who believe in the Trinity become irrelevant when one simply reviews the numerous uncontested historical facts relating to how the Trinity, as a doctrine took shape during the 4th to 6th centuries. The actual language of the Trinity is lifted from Hellenic sources—in their philosophical discussions of substance, soul, mind and spirit—and from the language of the already existing and abundant trinities and triads amongst Pagan nations, chief amongst them the Solar or Sun Trinities of ancient Egypt. Thus, we have Nimrod, Tammuz and Semiramis (Babylon); Osiris, Horus and Isis (Egypt); Zeus, Apollo and Athena (Greece); Brahma, Vishnu and Shivu (India). Sun-worship featured heavily in these mystery religions and it should come as no surprise then that the Trinity appeared in the specific empire that it did: sun-worshipping pagan Rome.

Jesus in Islām

The Qurʾān notes the contention between the Jews and Christians regarding Jesus and the differing the Christians fell into regarding the status of Jesus shortly after his ascent. The Qurʾān clarifies the truth of that wherein they differed. In this chapter we provide an overview of the status of Jesus in Islām and the next chapter will look in more detail at the mention of Jesus and Mary in the Qurʾān.

Jesus (عَلَيْهِ السَّلَام) Son of Mary (عَلَيْهَا السَّلَام) is a righteous prophet from a line of Prophets including Abraham, Moses, David and Solomon. He was miraculously born of a chaste and righteous woman through Allāh's **spoken word** [of command] ("Be!") which instructed Gabriel to breathe of a **created spirit** into Mary through which Jesus was conceived and born.

إِنَّمَا ٱلْمَسِيحُ عِيسَى ٱبْنُ مَرْيَمَ رَسُولُ ٱللَّهِ وَكَلِمَتُهُۥٓ أَلْقَىٰهَآ إِلَىٰ مَرْيَمَ وَرُوحٌ مِّنْهُ

The Messiah, Jesus, the son of Mary, was but a messenger of Allāh and His word which He directed to Mary and a spirit [created at a command] from Him." (4:171).

Hence, Jesus is **the Word and the Spirit of Allāh** in the sense explained: created through Allāh's uncreated word of command for the sending of a spirit to serve as the mechanism for his conception without any male intervention. As confirmation of his prophethood, he spoke whilst in the cradle to defend his mother from calumny, healed the sick and raised the dead. He came to confirm the Torah (the law) and preach the Gospel (the news).

وَيُعَلِّمُهُ ٱلْكِتَٰبَ وَٱلْحِكْمَةَ وَٱلتَّوْرَىٰةَ وَٱلْإِنجِيلَ

"**And He [Allāh] will teach him the Book and the Wisdom and the Torah and the Gospel. And [make him] a messenger to the Children of Israel.**" (3:48).

The message of Jesus was not new or unique: salvation through worshipping Allāh alone, which is pure monotheism in belief and deed, and perfection of morals and character through adherence to the law and righteous works. As Jesus stated:

إِنَّ ٱللَّهَ رَبِّى وَرَبُّكُمْ فَٱعْبُدُوهُ هَٰذَا صِرَٰطٌ مُّسْتَقِيمٌ

"[Jesus]: Indeed, Allāh is my Lord and your Lord, so worship Him. That is the straight path." (3:51).

Jesus is among the greatest of all Prophets and is highly respected in Islām. A Muslim's faith is invalid without belief in Jesus.[58] Muslims are in fact the true followers of Jesus today, just as they are the true followers of Moses.[59] Prophet Muḥammad (ﷺ) said: "*Both in this world and the next, I am the nearest of all the people to the Son of Mary, and all the prophets are paternal brothers, and there has been no prophet*

---

[58] By *name*, Moses is mentioned over 120 times in the Qur'ān, Jesus around twenty-five and Muḥammad (ﷺ) four times, indicating the status that Moses and Jesus have in Islām. Had Muḥammad (ﷺ) been the author of the Qur'ān his own name would have been mentioned more frequently and made much more prominent. Allāh (عَزَّوَجَلَّ) stated:

قُلْ مَا كُنتُ بِدْعًا مِّنَ ٱلرُّسُلِ وَمَآ أَدْرِى مَا يُفْعَلُ بِى وَلَا بِكُمْ إِنْ أَتَّبِعُ إِلَّا مَا يُوحَىٰٓ إِلَىَّ وَمَآ أَنَا۠ إِلَّا نَذِيرٌ مُّبِينٌ

"Say : 'I am not something original among the messengers, nor do I know what will be done with me or with you. I only follow that which is revealed to me, and I am not but a clear warner." (46:9).

Meaning, the message of Muḥammad (ﷺ) is a continuation of the message of the previous Prophets, who are given honourable mention, and Muḥammad (ﷺ) speaks not of his own accord but faithfully conveys what is revealed to him.

[59] As for what is known as Judaism today, it is not what Moses originally called to, Moses called to Islām (submission to Allāh with pure monotheism, singling Him out with all forms of worship), as did all the Prophets and Messengers. Judaism is named after the tribe of Judah, one of the twelve tribes of Israel. The Jewish Encyclopedia makes a distinction between the original Mosaic teachings and Rabbinic Judaism, a later development which has remained the main character of Judaism till today. The Jewish Encylopedia mentions that the Israelite faith underwent frequent changes throughout the ages. It was strongly affected and moulded by the beliefs and practices of host nations such as Egypt, Persia and Babylonia. The Qur'ān rehearsed to Jews in the era of Muḥammad (ﷺ) the great favours Allāh had bestowed upon the Children of Israel when they had been upon right guidance and were the best of nations. It reminded them how their religious leaders had departed from the guidance of Moses, altered their scripture and law, entered into the practice of sorcery, fell into polytheism, contended with their prophets and distorted the religion of Islām they were ordered to follow.

between me and him (Jesus)."[60] The Prophet also said: "*Whoever testifies that no deity is worthy of worship but Allāh alone, without any partners, that Muḥammad is His servant and Messenger, that Jesus is the servant of Allāh, His Word which He bestowed upon Mary, a Spirit from Him, and that Paradise is true and Hellfire is true, then he will enter Paradise through any of the eight gates of Paradise he wishes.*"[61]

Regarding the statement of Allāh (عَزَّوَجَلَّ):

يَٰٓأَهْلَ ٱلْكِتَٰبِ لَا تَغْلُوا۟ فِى دِينِكُمْ وَلَا تَقُولُوا۟ عَلَى ٱللَّهِ إِلَّا ٱلْحَقَّ إِنَّمَا ٱلْمَسِيحُ
عِيسَى ٱبْنُ مَرْيَمَ رَسُولُ ٱللَّهِ وَكَلِمَتُهُۥٓ أَلْقَىٰهَآ إِلَىٰ مَرْيَمَ وَرُوحٌ مِّنْهُ فَـَٔامِنُوا۟ بِٱللَّهِ
وَرُسُلِهِۦ وَلَا تَقُولُوا۟ ثَلَٰثَةٌ ٱنتَهُوا۟ خَيْرًا لَّكُمْ إِنَّمَا ٱللَّهُ إِلَٰهٌ وَٰحِدٌ سُبْحَٰنَهُۥٓ أَن يَكُونَ لَهُۥ
وَلَدٌ لَّهُۥ مَا فِى ٱلسَّمَٰوَٰتِ وَمَا فِى ٱلْأَرْضِ وَكَفَىٰ بِٱللَّهِ وَكِيلًا

"O People of the Scripture, do not commit excess in your religion and nor say about Allah except the truth. The Messiah, Jesus, the son of Mary, was but a messenger of Allāh and His word which He directed to Mary and a soul [created at a command] from Him. So believe in Allāh and His messengers. And do not say, 'Three'. Desist, it is better for you. Indeed, Allāh is but one God. Exalted is He above having a son. To Him belongs whatever is in the heavens and whatever is on the earth. And sufficient is Allāh as Disposer of affairs." (4:171).

This verse was revealed in relation to various factions of the Christians. They had sayings such as, "*Jesus is Allāh*", "*He is the son of Allāh*" and "*He is the third of three.*" The commentators of the Qur'ān provide the following general elaboration of the meaning of the above verse, as clarification and admonition for Christians:

"O people of the Gospel, do not exceed the true belief and do not exaggerate and say of Allāh except the truth. Do not claim a son and wife for Him, for Jesus the son of Mary was no more than a messenger like many other messengers before him. He was sent with the message of Islām which is to worship Allāh alone, without ascribing any partners to Him. [The ability to recognize this truth is part of an innate disposition and natural instinct—the *fiṭrah*—which

[60] Reported by Imām al-Bukhāri in his Ṣaḥīḥ.
[61] Reported by Imām Muslim in his Ṣaḥīḥ.

every person is born with]. Just like this truth also attested to by the wonders and signs in creation.

So Jesus is the Messenger of Allāh. He is the Word of Allāh, with the meaning that he was created through a Word spoken by Allāh which is 'Be!'—not that he, Jesus, in his essence, is the actual Word of Allāh. It was through this Word that Gabriel (*Jibrīl*) was sent and he breathed from the Spirit (*Rūḥ*) of Allāh into Mary (عَلَيْهَاٱلسَّلَامُ). This Spirit is not a part of Allāh's essence but a created entity which gave rise to life and its reality is unknown. The same Spirit was breathed into Ādam (عَلَيْهِٱلسَّلَامُ) who was born without father and mother. Through this Spirit came the miraculous birth of Jesus.

Hence, Jesus is the Word and the Spirit of Allāh. He was created through Allāh's Word of command and the sending and breathing of the created Spirit through Jibrīl. So people of the Gospel, believe in this truth regarding Jesus, the Son of Mary and submit to Allāh alone. Shun the worship of all other deities including Jesus and his mother Mary and do not say '*There are three*,' for Allāh is only one deity who is worthy of worship in truth.

You have unjustly raised Jesus from the station of prophethood and messengership to one of lordship (*rububiyyah*). Yet Jesus and his mother Mary were mere mortals, they ate, drank and walked the Earth and owned and controlled nothing in the heavens and Earth, save that Allāh bestowed miracles upon Jesus as a sign of his prophethood. Desist from this statement of 'Three,' believe in the absolute oneness of Allāh and worship only Him alone. This is the straight path indicated by authentic, uncorrupted revelation and sound reason."[62]

The next chapter looks in a bit more detail at Jesus and Mary in the Noble Qur'ān.

---

[62] Refer to the exegesis of Ibn Kathīr, al-Ṭabarī and al-Baghawi.

Jesus and Mary in the Qur'ān

The position of Jesus (عَلَيْهِ السَّلَامُ) and his mother Maryam (عَلَيْهَا السَّلَامُ) is a very lofty one in the Qur'ān. It contrasts with their portrayal in Talmudic literature. One is a Messenger and Prophet of Allāh, and the other, his mother, a *siddīqah* (extremely truthful in intention, word and deed), a title given to those from mankind who attain the best possible rank short of prophethood.

The 19th chapter of the Qur'ān is named after Mary and verses 16 to 36 relate to the conception and birth of Jesus. Any translation—no matter how good and accurate—cannot do justice to the rhythmic beauty, eloquence and power of the Arabic original. Similarly, her story and that of Jesus is mentioned in the 3rd chapter titled "The Family of ʿĪmrān" between verses 35 and 60. Mention is also made of Jesus and his helpers at the end of the 5th chapter titled "The Table Spread", between verses 110 and 120.[63]

The Honourable Mention of Mary in the Qur'ān.

Allāh (عَزَّوَجَلَّ) said:

وَٱذْكُرْ فِى ٱلْكِتَٰبِ مَرْيَمَ إِذِ ٱنتَبَذَتْ مِنْ أَهْلِهَا مَكَانًا شَرْقِيًّا

"And mention, [O Muḥammad], in the Book [the story of] Mary, when she withdrew from her family to a place toward the east." (19:16).

Allāh has honoured Mary the mother of Jesus tremendously in that she has been given lofty mention in the Qur'ān. The Muslims have been ordered to remember her and her story. This Qur'ān is read across the east and west by hundreds of millions of people. They recite, in rhythmic tones, and mention the virtues of Mary, her chastity, her piety, her devotion, her being chosen over all the other women of the world.

The mention of Mary and her son Jesus brings tears to their eyes, as they recite or listen to the various heart-wrenching, tear-jerking

---

[63] Most of the commentary in this section has been summarised from *Taysīr al-Karīm al-Raḥmān* (Beirut: Muʿassasah al-Risālah, 2002) of Shaykh ʿAbd al-Raḥmān bin Nāṣir al-Saʿdī (d. 1956).

accounts in the Qur'ān and they experience these feelings upon sound knowledge, historical truth and justice.

Mary's Seclusion and Devotion to Allāh.

Allāh (عَزَّوَجَلَّ) said:

فَٱتَّخَذَتْ مِن دُونِهِمْ حِجَابًا فَأَرْسَلْنَآ إِلَيْهَا رُوحَنَا فَتَمَثَّلَ لَهَا بَشَرًا سَوِيًّا

"And she took, in seclusion from them, a screen. Then We sent to her our spirit [Gabriel], and he appeared before her in the form of a man in all respects." (19:17).

Mary went in seclusion from her family, to a place in the east and took a screen for herself. The reason for this was so that she could focus on worshipping her Lord in a state of sincerity, humility and submission. Due to her intense desire to protect her chastity, Allāh favoured her by bestowing her a son without any male intervention. Thus, Allāh sent Gabriel who appeared to her in the form of a man possessing excellent stature, utmost beauty, and absence of any flaws in appearance to give her glad tidings.

Mary's Modesty and Chastity.

Allāh (عَزَّوَجَلَّ) said:

قَالَتْ إِنِّىٓ أَعُوذُ بِٱلرَّحْمَٰنِ مِنكَ إِن كُنتَ تَقِيًّا قَالَ إِنَّمَآ أَنَا رَسُولُ رَبِّكِ لِأَهَبَ لَكِ غُلَٰمًا زَكِيًّا قَالَتْ أَنَّىٰ يَكُونُ لِى غُلَٰمٌ وَلَمْ يَمْسَسْنِى بَشَرٌ وَلَمْ أَكُ بَغِيًّا قَالَ كَذَٰلِكِ قَالَ رَبُّكِ هُوَ عَلَىَّ هَيِّنٌ وَلِنَجْعَلَهُۥٓ ءَايَةً لِّلنَّاسِ وَرَحْمَةً مِّنَّا وَكَانَ أَمْرًا مَّقْضِيًّا

"She said, 'Indeed, I seek refuge in the Most Merciful from you, [so leave me], if you do fear Allāh.' He said, 'I am only the messenger of your Lord to give you [news of] a pure, righteous son.' She said, 'How can I have a son when no man has touched me and nor am I unchaste?' He said, 'Thus [it shall be]. Your Lord says, 'It is easy for Me, and We will make him a sign to the people and a mercy from Us. And it is a matter [already] decreed'.'" (19:18-21).

When Mary saw him—and she was in isolation, away from her family, and had taken a screen for privacy—she feared that this man may intend evil. So she sought refuge in Allāh, the Most-Merciful and admonished the man, thereby combining between two matters:

holding fast to her Lord by seeking protection and admonishing the man to have fear of Allāh. This is evidence of her utmost modesty and chastity—in that she protected her chastity despite the circumstances which invited to contrary behaviour—and it is also a refutation of the calumny of the calumniators who later attacked her honour. Due to her chastity, Allāh, granted her a son who would be a sign from amongst His signs.

When Gabriel saw her fear and concern, he informed her that he is merely a messenger from his Lord to inform her and convey the message to her that Allāh is going to bestow her a pure [blameless, faultless], righteous child, possessing praiseworthy qualities. This surprised her and she asked as to how she could give birth to a son without being touched by a man. She was informed by Gabriel that Allāh had decreed such a matter because it is easy for Him. This indicates that all natural laws and cause-effect mechanisms do not function independently and are subject to Allāh's creative power, His decree and determination. Allāh is able to alter them or bypass them and in this case, out of His favour and bounty, He granted Mary a son without the intervention of any man.

This was also a display of mercy (*raḥmah*) in that Allāh made this son to be a prophet and messenger, one who would recite His verses, instruct them in the Book and Wisdom, thereby purifying them and leading them to happiness and felicity in both this life and the next.

Allāh makes mention of Mary's chastity in another place:

وَالَّتِي أَحْصَنَتْ فَرْجَهَا فَنَفَخْنَا فِيهَا مِن رُّوحِنَا وَجَعَلْنَاهَا وَابْنَهَا آيَةً لِّلْعَالَمِينَ

"And (remember) she [the virgin Mary] who guarded her chastity, We breathed into her [through our Spirit, Gabriel], and We made her and her son [Jesus] a sign for the worlds (of men and jinn)." (21:91).

The meaning of this verse is explained by scholars of Qur'ānic exegesis (*tafsīr*) as follows:[64]

Remember Mary who is being praised, whose lofty status is being explained, and whose nobility is being announced, the one who

---

[64] Summarised from the explanations and commentaries of al-Ṭabari, Ibn Kathir, al-Baghawī, al-Sa'dī and al-Muyassar.

preserved her innocence and virginity by maintaining utmost chastity by safeguarding herself from what is unlawful and shunning everything that brings one closer to what is unlawful [in terms of sexual relations]. She even guarded herself from what was lawful, thereby not marrying due to being preoccupied and engrossed in worship, remembrance, chastity and serving her Lord. As a reward for her utmost piety and chastity, Allāh (عَزَّوَجَلَّ) rewarded her by bestowing upon her a son without the intervention of any male. Hence, she was able to maintain her chastity which she had piously and diligently guarded. Gabriel was sent to give her glad tidings and he came with the Spirit [a created entity whose reality is unknown] which was breathed into her, leading her to conceive, by the permission of Allāh. Both Mary and Jesus were made a sign for the worlds [of jinn and men]. Mary gave birth without male intervention and Jesus spoke as an infant. Miracles were made to occur through him such that generations after generations would make mention of Jesus (and his mother), and such that they come to know that Allāh is powerful over all things, and that from His far-reaching wisdom is that He creates whatever and however He wills.

The Birth of Jesus.

Allāh (عَزَّوَجَلَّ) said:

فَحَمَلَتْهُ فَٱنتَبَذَتْ بِهِۦ مَكَانًا قَصِيًّا. فَأَجَآءَهَا ٱلْمَخَاضُ إِلَىٰ جِذْعِ ٱلنَّخْلَةِ قَالَتْ يَٰلَيْتَنِى مِتُّ قَبْلَ هَٰذَا وَكُنتُ نَسْيًا مَّنسِيًّا. فَنَادَىٰهَا مِن تَحْتِهَآ أَلَّا تَحْزَنِى قَدْ جَعَلَ رَبُّكِ تَحْتَكِ سَرِيًّا. وَهُزِّىٓ إِلَيْكِ بِجِذْعِ ٱلنَّخْلَةِ تُسَٰقِطْ عَلَيْكِ رُطَبًا جَنِيًّا. فَكُلِى وَٱشْرَبِى وَقَرِّى عَيْنًا فَإِمَّا تَرَيِنَّ مِنَ ٱلْبَشَرِ أَحَدًا فَقُولِىٓ إِنِّى نَذَرْتُ لِلرَّحْمَٰنِ صَوْمًا فَلَنْ أُكَلِّمَ ٱلْيَوْمَ إِنسِيًّا

"So she conceived him, and she withdrew with him to a far place. And the pains of childbirth drove her to the trunk of a date-palm. She said, 'Oh, I wish I had died before this and was in oblivion, forgotten.' But he [an angel] called her from below her, 'Do not grieve. Your Lord has provided beneath you a water stream. And shake toward you the trunk of the palm tree; it will drop upon you ripe, fresh dates. So eat and drink and be contented. And if you see

any human being, say, 'Indeed, I have vowed to the Most Merciful abstention, so I will not speak today to [any] human being.'" (19:22-26).

When she was made to conceive [through Gabriel blowing into her of the created spirit he was sent with], she feared scorn and rebuke from her people, and withdrew to a far place. She suffered numerous types of pain, both physical and emotional: the pains of childbirth and the pains of what the people would say, accusing her of immoral conduct of which she was completely innocent. Unable to bear these pains she wished she had died before this event in her life and had been a thing forgotten. However, an angel comforted her and instructed her not to grieve and to take from the stream and the dates which would provide relief to her. And as for her other pain, the pain of what people would say to her, the angel instructed her to not to speak to anyone, vowing silence. By not speaking to them, she would be saved from the grief created by their speech, since they would not believe her in any case. Rather, she would be exonerated by her own son, which is the greatest testimony of her innocence. Since bringing a son in this manner was out of the ordinary, then evidence of her innocence and her utmost chastity would also have to be out of the ordinary.

Mary Brings Jesus to Her People.

Allāh (عَزَّوَجَلَّ) said:

فَأَتَتْ بِهِۦ قَوْمَهَا تَحْمِلُهُۥ قَالُوا۟ يَـٰمَرْيَمُ لَقَدْ جِئْتِ شَيْـًٔا فَرِيًّا. يَـٰٓأُخْتَ هَـٰرُونَ مَا كَانَ أَبُوكِ ٱمْرَأَ سَوْءٍ وَمَا كَانَتْ أُمُّكِ بَغِيًّا

"Then she brought him to her people, carrying him. They said, 'O Mary, you have certainly done a thing unprecedented. O sister of Aaron, your father was not a man who used to commit adultery, nor was your mother an unchaste woman'." (19:27-28).

When her postnatal period had ended, Mary returned to her people, carrying Jesus, with her knowledge that she is totally pure and innocent. Hence, she came without care and concern. They told her that she had brought an enormity, something without precedent, and what they really meant was that she was guilty of immorality. They protested to her by referring to her as the sister of Aaron,[65] and stating that her parents were upright people, free and innocent of this type of immoral act of which she stood accused. This indicates, incidentally, their understanding that children generally acquire the ways and behaviours of their parents. So Mary had to exonerate herself from the grievous charge of which she stood accused by her people.

Jesus's Defence of his Mother and Statement of Prophethood.

Allāh (عَزَّوَجَلَّ) said:

فَأَشَارَتْ إِلَيْهِ قَالُواْ كَيْفَ نُكَلِّمُ مَن كَانَ فِي ٱلْمَهْدِ صَبِيًّا. قَالَ إِنِّي عَبْدُ ٱللَّهِ ءَاتَىٰنِيَ ٱلْكِتَٰبَ وَجَعَلَنِي نَبِيًّا. وَجَعَلَنِي مُبَارَكًا أَيْنَ مَا كُنتُ وَأَوْصَٰنِي بِٱلصَّلَوٰةِ وَٱلزَّكَوٰةِ مَا دُمْتُ حَيًّا. وَبَرًّۢا بِوَٰلِدَتِي وَلَمْ يَجْعَلْنِي جَبَّارًا شَقِيًّا وَٱلسَّلَٰمُ عَلَيَّ يَوْمَ وُلِدتُّ وَيَوْمَ أَمُوتُ وَيَوْمَ أُبْعَثُ حَيًّا

---

[65] Aaron was the name given to righteous people amongst the Children of Israel, because there used to be a man amongst them called Aaron who was very righteous. So when Mary brought the baby, they said to her "*O sister of Aaron*", meaning "*O one associated with righteousness*" because she came from a righteous family. The Muslim scholar of Qur'ānic explanation, Imām al-Ṭabari (d. 923) mentions this view from Qatādah (an early commentator of the Qur'ān who studied with the Prophet's companions), Muḥammad bin Sīrīn (another early Muslim scholar) and others. Another Qur'ān scholar, Imām al-Baghawi (d. 1122) mentioned that Qatādah and others explained that Aaron was a righteous worshipper and that forty-thousand people followed his funeral the day that he died, all of them called Aaron. This name was associated with piety and righteousness and hence, the phrase "*O sister of Aaron*" is not referring to blood relationship. This is like the statement of Allāh, "**Verily, the spendthrifts (those who squander wealth) are the brethren of the devils...**" (17:27). Imām al-Baghawi also cites a narration from al-Kalbī that the Aaron referred to here was a brother of Mary through her father, and he was the most righteous man amongst the Children of Israel in that time. Imām Ibn Kathir (d. 1373) supports this view and cites from Imām al-Tabari in this regard. And Imām al-Sa'dī (d. 1956) from the contemporary Muslim scholars also supports the view that this statement is referring to an actual brother of Mary called Aaron, and that the Children of Israel used to call their children by the names of former prophets.

"So she pointed to him. They said, 'How can we speak to one who is in the cradle a child?' [Jesus] said, 'Indeed, I am the servant of Allāh. He has given me the Scripture and made me a prophet. And He has made me blessed wherever I am and has enjoined upon me prayer and charity (zakāh) as long as I remain alive. And [He made me] dutiful to my mother, and has not made me insolent, unblessed. And peace is on me the day I was born and the day I will die and the day I am raised alive'." (19:29-33).

So Mary—having already vowed not to speak to the people—simply pointed to her child, hinting that they should speak to the child. Her people were surprised at this and asked as to how could they possibly speak to a child still in the cradle. Thereupon, Jesus spoke and informed them that he is a servant (*'abd*) of Allāh who will be given the Book and be made a prophet.

Hence, the first description of himself was that he was a servant and worshipper of Allāh, in servitude to Him, a refutation of those who deified Jesus and made him divine. Jesus denied having any attribute or quality that made him divine in his very first words. He then informed them of a second quality, which is that he will be made blessed wherever he may be. Meaning, that wherever he will be, he will be teaching others, inviting others to Allāh, to worship Him alone, instructing them, purifying them and bringing about benefit through his speech and action such that anyone and everyone who sat with him will acquire benefit and blessing.

Jesus, then informed them that he is commanded with prayer and charity so long as he lives. This is a second refutation of those who made him divine and worshipped him as a deity alongside Allāh. Through his first words, he mentioned that he would be constant in prayer to his Lord, proving that he is a worshipper and not the one worshipped. Thereafter, Jesus informed of a third matter which is that he has been ordered to show beautiful and righteous conduct with his mother, Mary. To show her utmost benevolence and to fulfil her rights.

Then he informed them that he is not one who is arrogant and despotic, unblessed and wretched in this life and the next. Rather, he is a humble, obedient, servant of Allāh, humble also towards Allāh's servants, pleased in this life and the next.

Finally, Jesus invoked peace upon himself, mentioning the bounty of Allāh upon him in that He granted him safety and peace on the day that he was born, and will do so on the day that he will eventually die [after his return] and the day that he shall be resurrected [along with the rest of humanity].

❧ The Teachings and Miracles of Jesus.

Allāh (عَزَّوَجَلَّ) said:

وَيُعَلِّمُهُ ٱلْكِتَـٰبَ وَٱلْحِكْمَةَ وَٱلتَّوْرَىٰةَ وَٱلْإِنجِيلَ. وَرَسُولًا إِلَىٰ بَنِىٓ إِسْرَٰٓءِيلَ أَنِّى قَدْ جِئْتُكُم بِـَٔايَةٍ مِّن رَّبِّكُمْ أَنِّىٓ أَخْلُقُ لَكُم مِّنَ ٱلطِّينِ كَهَيْـَٔةِ ٱلطَّيْرِ فَأَنفُخُ فِيهِ فَيَكُونُ طَيْرًۢا بِإِذْنِ ٱللَّهِ وَأُبْرِئُ ٱلْأَكْمَهَ وَٱلْأَبْرَصَ وَأُحْىِ ٱلْمَوْتَىٰ بِإِذْنِ ٱللَّهِ وَأُنَبِّئُكُم بِمَا تَأْكُلُونَ وَمَا تَدَّخِرُونَ فِى بُيُوتِكُمْ إِنَّ فِى ذَٰلِكَ لَءَايَةً لَّكُمْ إِن كُنتُم مُّؤْمِنِينَ. وَمُصَدِّقًا لِّمَا بَيْنَ يَدَىَّ مِنَ ٱلتَّوْرَىٰةِ وَلِأُحِلَّ لَكُم بَعْضَ ٱلَّذِى حُرِّمَ عَلَيْكُمْ وَجِئْتُكُم بِـَٔايَةٍ مِّن رَّبِّكُمْ فَٱتَّقُوا۟ ٱللَّهَ وَأَطِيعُونِ. إِنَّ ٱللَّهَ رَبِّى وَرَبُّكُمْ فَٱعْبُدُوهُ هَـٰذَا صِرَٰطٌ مُّسْتَقِيمٌ

"And He [Allāh] will teach him [Jesus] the Book and the Wisdom, the Torah and the Gospel. And [make him] a messenger to the Children of Israel, [who will say]: 'Indeed I have come to you with a sign from your Lord in that I design for you from clay [that which is] like the form of a bird, then I breathe into it and it becomes a bird by permission of Allāh. And I cure the blind and the leper, and I give life to the dead by permission of Allāh . And I inform you of what you eat and what you store in your houses. Indeed in that is a sign for you, if you are believers. And [I have come] confirming what was before me of the Torah and to make lawful for you some of what was forbidden to you. And I have come to you with a sign from your Lord, so fear Allāh and obey me. Indeed, Allāh is my Lord and your Lord, so worship Him. That is the straight path'." (3:48-51).

Allāh taught Jesus (عَلَيْهِ ٱلسَّلَامُ) that which was in past revealed books, collectively referred to as "the Book", made him a messenger to the Children of Israel, and supported him with signs. From those signs was that Jesus designed and formed a bird from clay, breathed into it, rendering it a living bird by Allāh's permission. He would also cure the blind and the leper, and give life to the dead, all by Allāh's permission. Jesus would also inform them of things only they knew and he could not possibly have known, such as what they ate and stored in their houses [at particular times and occasions]. All of these were signs and Jesus mentioned these signs to them as proof of his messengership, so that they would listen to him and obey him and his teachings, which are not new, but merely a confirmation of that which was taught by Moses (عَلَيْهِ ٱلسَّلَامُ) before him, before it had been altered.

Thus, Allāh strengthened Jesus with two types of proof:

- the first, in the form of signs (miracles)
- the second, revelation.

The revelation, the Gospel, was a confirmation of the Torah, a clear indication that he was being truthful. For if Jesus was lying, he would have invented what would be contrary to the teachings of previous prophets, and would have opposed the foundations and branches of the Torah. Rather, he came to affirm the Torah and to make lawful for them what they had made unlawful upon themselves, to release them from the shackles of observance they had invented and imposed, extraneous to the original Torah.

Through these affairs: various signs and miracles, corroboration of the original Mosaic law, releasing them from their self-imposed shackles and teaching wisdom, he called them with the call of all the Messengers: To single out Allāh in worship exclusive to all other deities; to worship Him through what He legislated and commanded; and to abandon all extraneous additions. He informed them that this is the straight path which leads to Allāh, and none other.

However the religious elders and leaders, the chiefs and priests of the Pharisees, resented his challenge to their authority, his rejection of their distortion of the law and his condemnation of their iniquities and excesses. Seeing Jesus as a threat to the "national existence", they plotted to kill him after accusing him of blasphemy, and desecration of the Torah.

These tribulations were like the tribulations of previous Prophets who had been oppressed and harmed in the cause of truth.

Jesus Was not Killed nor Crucified.

The leaders of those who rejected Jesus hatched plots to kill and crucify him, and just as they plotted, Allāh too plotted against them.

Allāh (عَزَّوَجَلَّ) said:

إِذْ قَالَ اللَّهُ يَا عِيسَىٰ إِنِّي مُتَوَفِّيكَ وَرَافِعُكَ إِلَيَّ وَمُطَهِّرُكَ مِنَ الَّذِينَ كَفَرُوا وَجَاعِلُ الَّذِينَ اتَّبَعُوكَ فَوْقَ الَّذِينَ كَفَرُوا إِلَىٰ يَوْمِ الْقِيَامَةِ ثُمَّ إِلَيَّ مَرْجِعُكُمْ فَأَحْكُمُ بَيْنَكُمْ فِيمَا كُنتُمْ فِيهِ تَخْتَلِفُونَ

"[Mention] when Allāh said: 'O Jesus, indeed I will take you and raise you to Myself and purify you from those who disbelieve and make those who follow you [in submission to Allāh alone] superior to those who disbelieve until the Day of Resurrection. Then to Me is your return, and I will judge between you concerning that in which you used to differ'." (3:55).

Allāh informed Jesus that He will raise and purify him of those who unjustly claimed he is Allāh's son. Likewise, He informed him that He will purify him of those who rejected and slandered him and accused him and his mother of enormities. He also informed that those who follow Jesus in pure monotheism and observance of law—and who accept Muḥammad (صَلَّى ٱللَّهُ عَلَيْهِ وَسَلَّمَ) who was foretold by Jesus—that they will be uppermost and dominant against those who reject his prophethood until the Day of Judgement.

Allāh (عَزَّوَجَلَّ) also said:

وَقَوْلِهِمْ إِنَّا قَتَلْنَا الْمَسِيحَ عِيسَى ابْنَ مَرْيَمَ رَسُولَ اللَّهِ وَمَا قَتَلُوهُ وَمَا صَلَبُوهُ وَلَٰكِن شُبِّهَ لَهُمْ وَإِنَّ الَّذِينَ اخْتَلَفُوا فِيهِ لَفِي شَكٍّ مِّنْهُ مَا لَهُم بِهِ مِنْ عِلْمٍ إِلَّا اتِّبَاعَ الظَّنِّ وَمَا قَتَلُوهُ يَقِينًا . بَل رَّفَعَهُ اللَّهُ إِلَيْهِ وَكَانَ اللَّهُ عَزِيزًا حَكِيمًا

"And [for] their saying, 'Indeed, we have killed the Messiah, Jesus, the son of Mary, the messenger of Allāh.' And they did not kill him, nor did they crucify him; but [another] was made to resemble him to them. And indeed, those who differ over it are in doubt about it. They have no knowledge of it except the following of assumption. And they did not kill him, for certain. Rather, Allāh raised him to Himself. And ever is Allāh Exalted in Might and Wise." (4:157-158).

They did not kill or crucify Jesus. Rather, it was made to appear to them as such. With respect to his alleged death, both the Jews and Christians are in confusion, bewilderment and doubt, speaking with conjectures and untruths. They do not have sure knowledge in these affairs, and much confusion arises out of their scripture.

In the Prophetic traditions, Jesus will return prior to the Day of Judgement, clarify the truth and judge by Islām. He will destroy the cross and kill the [unclean] swine and marry and have children. All of the People of the Book will believe in him before his death.

The Truth Regarding the Status of Jesus and his Call.

Allāh (عَزَّوَجَلَّ) said:

ذَٰلِكَ عِيسَى ٱبْنُ مَرْيَمَ قَوْلَ ٱلْحَقِّ ٱلَّذِى فِيهِ يَمْتَرُونَ. مَا كَانَ لِلَّهِ أَن يَتَّخِذَ مِن وَلَدٍ سُبْحَٰنَهُۥٓ إِذَا قَضَىٰٓ أَمْرًا فَإِنَّمَا يَقُولُ لَهُۥ كُن فَيَكُونُ. وَإِنَّ ٱللَّهَ رَبِّى وَرَبُّكُمْ فَٱعْبُدُوهُ هَٰذَا صِرَٰطٌ مُّسْتَقِيمٌ

"That is Jesus, the son of Mary, [and it is] the word of truth about which they are in dispute. It is not [befitting] for Allāh to take a son, exalted and sublime is He! When He decrees an affair, He only says to it, 'Be,' and it is. [Jesus said], 'And indeed, Allāh is my Lord and your Lord, so worship Him. This is a straight path'." (19:34-36).

The reality of Jesus is as he described himself. A humble servant of Allāh, bestowed with prophethood, devoted to prayer and charity, righteous to his mother, a caller and teacher to goodness. This is the undisputed, historical word of truth and as for all other claims—whether those of the Jews or Christians—they are all conjectures, doubts, lies and fabrications. Hence, their disputes with each other on this issue. Thus, some of them say Jesus is Allāh, others say he is the son of Allāh, others say he is the third of three, and all of these are lies. Similarly, what the Jews accused him and his mother of are all calumnies, fabrications.

Allāh refutes the Christians by stating that it is not befitting for Him to take a son as this is from the impossible affairs. He is free of all needs (*al-Ghaniyy*), worthy of all praise (*al-Ḥamīd*), the owner and master (*al-Mālik*) of everything. Thus, He does not take a son from His servants, He is sublime and glorified above that. But whenever

He desires an affair [such as the conception of a child without male intervention], then He simply says "Be!" and it is. Then Jesus informed his people that Allāh is his Lord and their Lord (*Rabb*) and thus, only He should be worshipped alone, since the two affairs are binding. Whoever affirms Allāh is his Lord—the one who creates, owns, provides, sustains, gives and takes life, heals, guides, misguides and so on—then it is binding upon him to single out Allāh in worship. This is the straight path, the path that all the previous Prophets and Messengers called to, and it is the only path that leads to Allāh and to His mercy and forgiveness.

Jesus Was no More than a Prophet and Messenger.

Allāh (عَزَّوَجَلَّ) said:

مَّا الْمَسِيحُ ابْنُ مَرْيَمَ إِلاَّ رَسُولٌ قَدْ خَلَتْ مِن قَبْلِهِ الرُّسُلُ وَأُمُّهُ صِدِّيقَةٌ كَانَا يَأْكُلاَنِ الطَّعَامَ انظُرْ كَيْفَ نُبَيِّنُ لَهُمُ الآيَاتِ ثُمَّ انظُرْ أَنَّى يُؤْفَكُونَ

"The Messiah [Jesus, son of Mary] was no more than a Messenger, many were the Messengers that passed away before him. His mother (Mary) was a *ṣiddīqah* [one who believes and is extremely truthful in intention, word and deed]. They both used to eat food. Look at how We make the signs clear to them, yet look at how they are deluded from the Truth." (5:75).

Both Jesus and his mother used to eat food, because they were in need of food and drink in order to sustain their bodies. Anyone who consumes food can never be a deity because he or she is dependent upon another and not self-sufficient. All people with sound innate disposition and basic common sense know full well that dependence upon food is a sign of incapacity and he who is not self-sufficient can never be a deity in truth. The Muslim scholar and commentator of the Qur'ān, Imām al-Baghawi (d. 1122), stated in his explanation of this verse that the mention of food here is an indirect expression of the passing of stool and urine, which means that anyone who ate and drank must necessarily pass stool and urine. How can the one characterized as such be a deity in truth? This is a subtle allusion to the futility of the claim that Jesus is divine. Allāh says, **"Look at how We make the signs clear to them, yet look at how they are deluded**

from the truth." An indication of how the Christians who deified Jesus and turned him into God are deluded, despite evident signs and proofs being made clear.

Jesus Was not Proud to be a Humble Servant.

Allāh (عَزَّوَجَلَّ) said:

لَن يَسْتَنكِفَ الْمَسِيحُ أَن يَكُونَ عَبْداً لِّلّهِ وَلاَ الْمَلآئِكَةُ الْمُقَرَّبُونَ وَمَن يَسْتَنكِفْ عَنْ عِبَادَتِهِ وَيَسْتَكْبِرْ فَسَيَحْشُرُهُمْ إِلَيهِ جَمِيعًا

"The Messiah will never be proud to reject being a slave to Allāh, nor the angels who are near [to Allāh]. And whosoever rejects His worship and is arrogant, then He will gather them all together unto Himself." (4:172).

When a delegation of Christians from Najrān [in southwestern Arabia] came to the Prophet Muḥammad (صَلَّاللَّهُعَلَيْهِوَسَلَّمَ), they said to him, "O Muḥammad, you belittle our companion (Jesus)," and they meant that in the Qur᾽ān he is referred to as a slave of Allāh (ʿAbd Allāh). The Prophet replied, "It is not a shortcoming for Jesus to be a slave of Allāh." This verse was then revealed. Jesus (عَلَيْهِالسَّلَامُ) did not scorn being a slave of Allāh, just as the near Angels do not scorn to be in servitude to Him. Jesus, like all the Prophets of goodness, were humble servants of Allāh who bowed and prostrated to Him in humility and worship.

This is in contrast to the Christians who exaggerated and gave him divine qualities, or from another angle, gave Allāh human qualities. Thus Jesus is mentioned in this verse—along with the near Angels who are in humble submission to their Lord—as a slave of Allāh. Jesus was desirous of worshipping his Lord, and this matter is preserved in the Gospels in which it is mentioned that Jesus would kneel, bow and fall on his face in prostration.

There occurs: "And he (Jesus) went a little farther, and fell on his face, and prayed."[66] Falling on his face means he prostrated.

Also: "In those days, Jesus went out to the mountain to pray, and He spent the night in prayer to God."[67] And also: "After He had sent

---

[66] Matthew 26:39.

the crowds away, He went up on the mountain by Himself to pray; and when it was evening, He was there alone."[68]

The worship of all of the Prophets of Children of Israel comprised both bowing and prostration in submission to their Lord. Prostration (*sujud*) is from the greatest aspects of prayer, others being bowing (*rukūʾ*), standing (*qiyām*), sitting (*julūs*) and invocation (*duʿā*). The Muslim prayer is comprised of all of these matters. It is the prayer of all of the Prophets of Allāh. Some details of this prayer can still be found in the Torah and Gospel, enough to recognize the similarities between it and the prayer of the Muslims who are the true followers of Jesus (عَلَيْهِ السَّلَامُ).

So this is the example of Jesus, a Prophet, a humble worshipper of Allāh from a line of Prophets sent to the Jews calling them to single out Allāh in worship and to abide by the Torah truthfully and faithfully. He was a mortal, both he and his mother ate and drank. His mother was favoured by Allāh for her utmost chastity, and was granted a son who would be from the greatest of messengers. Jesus and Mary were strict monotheists, given to devotion and worship of Allāh and they shunned the worship of other, false deities. This is Islām, the religion of Jesus and every prophet and messenger sent by Allāh (عَزَّوَجَلَّ). It is why Muslims, of all people, are closest to Jesus and have the greatest right to him.

Jesus Was a Muslim and His Message Was One of Peace (Salām) Through Submission to Allāh's Will.

All Muslims greet each other with the greeting of peace and safety. This is because Islām is to attain peace, serenity and safety through submission to Allāh's will upon pure monotheism. Hence, their greeting is one of peace and safety. No Prophet is mentioned except that Muslims invoke peace and safety upon him. The resemblance between Muslims and Jesus is very apparent, because in reality their religion and that of Jesus is one and the same. In Arabic, the word for peace and safety is *salām* and in Hebrew it is *shalom*.

---

[67] Luke 6:12.

[68] Matthew 14:23.

Muslims say, "*salām alaykum*" and Jesus would say "*shalom aleykhom*", both of which mean "*Peace and safety be upon you*".

We read the following in the Gospels:[69]

"And as they were still talking about this, Jesus himself stood in the midst of them, and said unto them, '*Peace be unto you*'." And: "And into whatsoever house ye enter, first say, '*Peace be to this house*'." And: "On the evening of that first day of the week, when the disciples were together, with the doors locked for fear of the Jews, Jesus came and stood among them and said, '*Peace be with you!*'" And: "Again Jesus said, '*Peace be with you!* As the Father has sent me, I am sending you'." And: "A week later his disciples were in the house again, and Thomas was with them. Though the doors were locked, Jesus came and stood among them and said, '*Peace be with you!*'"

The Christians do not invoke peace upon Jesus because they deified Him and made Him their Lord. But Muslims are true followers of the way of Jesus, in his speech, belief, greeting, prayer, worship and diet, rather even in his appearance and dress. Muslims believe in and worship only one true deity, consider Jesus a Prophet and Messiah and believe that salvation is through inward faith and outward works combined through adherence to the law. They are just as the true followers of Jesus were during his time.

The Split Between the Jews and Christians.

Allāh (عَزَّوَجَلَّ) said:

فَاخْتَلَفَ الْأَحْزَابُ مِن بَيْنِهِمْ فَوَيْلٌ لِّلَّذِينَ كَفَرُوا مِن مَّشْهَدِ يَوْمٍ عَظِيمٍ. أَسْمِعْ بِهِمْ وَأَبْصِرْ يَوْمَ يَأْتُونَنَا لَٰكِنِ الظَّالِمُونَ الْيَوْمَ فِي ضَلَالٍ مُّبِينٍ

"Then the factions differed [concerning Jesus] from among them, so woe to those who disbelieved from the scene of a tremendous Day. How [clearly] they will hear and see the Day they come to Us, but the wrongdoers today are in clear error." (19:37-38).

After Allāh explained the true status of Jesus the Son of Mary in which there is no doubt, He informed that the Jews and the Christians differed regarding him. In their various groups and sects,

---

[69] Refer to Luke 24:36, Luke 10:5, John 20:19, John 20:21 and John 20:26.

some fell into extremism and exaggeration and others fell into negligence. Hence, some said Jesus is Allāh, or the son of Allāh, or the third of three. Others rejected his prophethood and accused him of being an illegitimate child, born of an immoral woman and an idolator and magician. All of these are false statements built upon lies, conjectures and futile evidences and they are invalidated by the Qur'ān. Those holding such extremist views, at either end of the spectrum, Jews and Christians, are given a severe warning. They are reminded of the Final Day in which they will be resurrected and in which all creatures will be standing, in awe, awaiting judgement for their statements and deeds.

Repudiation of Christians for Deifying Jesus.

The Qur'ān repudiates the Christians for attributing divinity to Jesus, making him one of three, and for worshipping him and his mother—as is done by Catholics— alongside Allāh.

Allāh (عَزَّوَجَلَّ) stated:

لَّقَدْ كَفَرَ ٱلَّذِينَ قَالُوٓاْ إِنَّ ٱللَّهَ ثَالِثُ ثَلَٰثَةٍ وَمَا مِنْ إِلَٰهٍ إِلَّآ إِلَٰهٌ وَٰحِدٌ وَإِن لَّمْ يَنتَهُواْ عَمَّا يَقُولُونَ لَيَمَسَّنَّ ٱلَّذِينَ كَفَرُواْ مِنْهُمْ عَذَابٌ أَلِيمٌ. أَفَلَا يَتُوبُونَ إِلَى ٱللَّهِ وَيَسْتَغْفِرُونَهُۥ وَٱللَّهُ غَفُورٌ رَّحِيمٌ. مَّا ٱلْمَسِيحُ ٱبْنُ مَرْيَمَ إِلَّا رَسُولٌ قَدْ خَلَتْ مِن قَبْلِهِ ٱلرُّسُلُ وَأُمُّهُۥ صِدِّيقَةٌ كَانَا يَأْكُلَانِ ٱلطَّعَامَ ٱنظُرْ كَيْفَ نُبَيِّنُ لَهُمُ ٱلْءَايَٰتِ ثُمَّ ٱنظُرْ أَنَّىٰ يُؤْفَكُونَ. قُلْ أَتَعْبُدُونَ مِن دُونِ ٱللَّهِ مَا لَا يَمْلِكُ لَكُمْ ضَرًّا وَلَا نَفْعًا وَٱللَّهُ هُوَ ٱلسَّمِيعُ ٱلْعَلِيمُ.

"They have certainly disbelieved who say, 'Allāh is the third of three.' And there is no god [worthy of worship] except one God. And if they do not desist from what they are saying, there will surely afflict the disbelievers among them a painful punishment. So will they not repent to Allāh and seek His forgiveness? And Allāh is Forgiving and Merciful. The Messiah, son of Mary, was not but a messenger; [other] messengers have passed on before him. And his mother was a supporter of truth. They both used to eat food. Look how We make clear to them the signs; then look how they are deluded. Say, 'Do you worship besides Allāh that which holds for you

no [power of] harm or benefit while it is Allāh who is the Hearing, the Knowing?'." (5:73-76).

The Qur'ān does not ascribe a Trinitarian belief to all Christians, it merely refers to the disbelief of *those* who say "Allāh is one of three". Nor does it specifically define the Trinity anywhere. The formulation of the Trinity took centuries of debate and is an inherently confusing and contradictory idea, having no basis in authentic revelation, only in forged, inserted texts and interpolations.

The Christians are warned from such a saying and invited to repentance and seeking of forgiveness. After showing compassion to them by inviting them to right guidance, Allāh mentions the truth about the Jesus and his mother and gives them rational evidence why Jesus and his mother cannot be deities alongside Allāh. Despite these clear evidences, revealed and rational, and signs being made clear to them, they continue to ascribe divinity to Jesus, worshipping him alongside Allāh. Alongside reason and revelation, the now easily available factual historical record is another witness against them as it makes the evolution of Pauline Greco-Roman religion very clear: It is an obvious departure from the original "Jewish Christianity" led by Jesus's true followers, at the head of them James.

The Least Amount of Intelligence is Able to Distinguish Between Sound and Corrupt Doctrine.

The erudite Muslim scholar Ibn al-Qayyim (d. 1350) said: "How can the one who has the least amount of intelligence not distinguish between:

a) a religion whose foundation and building is erected upon worshipping the Most-Merciful [alone]; working for His love and pleasure with utmost sincerity in both secret and open; and behaving with people as He commanded, with [complete] justice and benevolence; whilst preferring His obedience to that of Satan,

and between:

b) a religion whose building is erected upon an undermined sand cliff ready to plunge a person straight into the Hellfire; one that is founded upon the worship of crosses and images engraved in ceilings and walls; [upon the belief] that the Lord of the Worlds descended from His Throne and occupied the womb of a female through which passes menstrual blood; that He remained therein for a period of time, in the darknesses of the womb, beneath the fat layer of the stomach, and then came out as a child suckled, growing gradually, crying, eating, drinking, urinating and sleeping, and meeting with other children; and then placed alongside the children of the Jews to learn what is desirable for a human [to learn]; and alongside this, He was circumcised; thereafter [upon implementing his mission] the Jews expelled Him and chased Him away from place to place and then captured Him, subjecting Him to various types of humiliation; thereafter they placed upon Him a crown of thorns, and carried Him onto a wooden crucifix whilst they were behind, in front of, and to the left and right of Him; then they dragged him in such a manner which makes the hearts quiver; then they tied His hands and feet with ropes and pinned them with nails that break the bones and tear the flesh, the while He is seeking rescue, 'O people have mercy upon me' and not a single person shows mercy to Him. And yet, [allegedly] this is the Controller of the universe, the upper and lower parts of it, the One invoked by all who are in the heavens and earth every day, and every day He [rules] by bringing about matters [in His creation], [whilst undergoing these humiliating affairs]! Then He dies, is buried in the dust beneath rocks and stones. He then rises from the dead to ascend back up to His Throne and His dominion after all that occurred. So what then do you think of the branches of the building that is built upon the likes of this foundation?!"[70]

The Christians claim that Allāh did all of this so that the sins of humanity can be forgiven. But this a revilement of Allāh, the Lord of the worlds, just as it is a revilement of intellect. Allāh forgives on account of repentance, seeking of forgiveness and righteous deeds. A forgiving, compassionate man does not need to throw his son in front of a lorry, or feed him to the sharks, and then say to his neighbours: "So long as you believe that I sacrificed my son's blood because I love you; and so long as you believe that my son died for your sins, so that I may forgive you, then you are pardoned and will

[70] *Hidāyat al-Ḥayārā Fī Ajwibat al-Yahūd wal-Naṣārā*. Dār ʿĀlam al-Fawāʾid (1429H) pp. 7-8.

receive salvation." To ascribe this to a rational human is a great insult. To ascribe it to the Lord of the worlds is an even greater insult of unfathomable proportions.

Ibn al-Qayyim also authored a poem titled "**O Christ-worshippers, we have a question**"[71] which appeals to a Christian's basic intuition and common sense. It is not subtle, but quite direct—because of the seriousness with which Muslims treat the association of partners with Allāh—and the essence of it can be summarised thus:

"O Christ-worshippers, we have a question! We desire its answer from the one who grasps it [among you]. When the Lord God died through the [intrigue] of a people who put him to death, then what kind of God is this? What they did to Him, did it please Him? If so, then glad tidings to them, for they certainly attained His [good] pleasure! If He was angered by what they did, then their strength overwhelmed His strength, [much to His displeasure]. And how were the hands of His enemies able to reach out and slap Him on the back of His neck? And did Christ bring himself [back to life] or was it a Life-giver, a Lord besides him? How strange it is, a grave that compressed God! And stranger still, a womb that confined Him! He remained therein for nine months, in darkness, nourished by blood! He was delivered as a small baby through the opening of a passage, weak and craving to be breast-fed! Did He eat and drink and do what they necessarily lead to [of passing stool and urine]? Is this a God? Lofty and exalted is Allāh from the lie fabricated by the Christians!

O Cross-worshippers! For what reason is it grave or repugnant to reject [the cross]? And do sound intellects but demand that it be broken and burned? Since the Lord God was carried on it unwillingly and His hands were fastened to it. What a cursed cross to carry in truth. So discard it and do not kiss it whenever you see it! The Lord of creation was demeaned upon it and yet you worship it! If you magnify it because it carried the Lord of all creatures, then He is exalted over that [which you ascribe to Him]."

Christians, both Arabs and non-Arabs, have claimed that this poem mischaracterises Christian beliefs and is based upon ignorance

---

[71] In his book *Ighāthat al-Lahafān Min Maṣāyid al-Shaytān.* Dār Ibn al-Jawzī (1420H) pp. 469-470.

regarding them. But these questions remain valid and are unaffected by the creative methods and explanations through which Christians might dismiss the rational and logical absurdities arising out of their conviction that Jesus is God incarnate. Worshipping Jesus as God and venerating the cross do not have any basis in *authentic scripture* nor in *sound intellect*. The earliest believers were "Jewish Christians" as has preceded, and these beliefs were completely unknown to them. They would have, without hesitation, considered them pure idolatry.

Repudiation of the Jews Who Slandered Mary.

The Qurʾān also repudiates the Jews who slandered Mary (عَلَيْهَا ٱلسَّلَامُ), rejected Jesus the Messiah, rejected his message and claimed to have killed him.

Allāh (عَزَّوَجَلَّ) stated:

وَبِكُفْرِهِمْ وَقَوْلِهِمْ عَلَىٰ مَرْيَمَ بُهْتَٰنًا عَظِيمًا. وَقَوْلِهِمْ إِنَّا قَتَلْنَا ٱلْمَسِيحَ عِيسَى ٱبْنَ
مَرْيَمَ رَسُولَ ٱللَّهِ وَمَا قَتَلُوهُ وَمَا صَلَبُوهُ وَلَٰكِن شُبِّهَ لَهُمْ وَإِنَّ ٱلَّذِينَ ٱخْتَلَفُوا۟ فِيهِ لَفِى
شَكٍّ مِّنْهُ مَا لَهُم بِهِۦ مِنْ عِلْمٍ إِلَّا ٱتِّبَاعَ ٱلظَّنِّ وَمَا قَتَلُوهُ يَقِينًۢا . بَل رَّفَعَهُ ٱللَّهُ إِلَيْهِ
وَكَانَ ٱللَّهُ عَزِيزًا حَكِيمًا. وَإِن مِّنْ أَهْلِ ٱلْكِتَٰبِ إِلَّا لَيُؤْمِنَنَّ بِهِۦ قَبْلَ مَوْتِهِۦ وَيَوْمَ ٱلْقِيَٰمَةِ
يَكُونُ عَلَيْهِمْ شَهِيدًا.

"And [We cursed them] for their disbelief and their saying against Mary a great slander. And [for] their saying, 'Indeed, we have killed the Messiah, Jesus, the son of Mary, the messenger of Allāh.' And they did not kill him, nor did they crucify him; but it was made to appear to them as such. And indeed, those who differ over it are in doubt regarding it. They have no knowledge of it except the following of assumption. And they did not kill him, for certain. Rather, Allāh raised him to Himself. And ever is Allāh Exalted in Might and Wise. And there is none from the People of the Scripture but that he will surely believe in Jesus before his death [when he returns]. And on the Day of Resurrection he will be against them a witness." (4:156-159.)

The status, honour, chastity and dignity of Mary is clarified by the Qurʾān elsewhere, and through it the vile slander against her is nullified and made of no effect. Mary was purified and chosen over all the women of the world (see Qur'ān 3:42). She was a chaste woman, devout and truthful in intentions, words and deeds.

What Jesus Will Say on the Day of Resurrection.

Allāh (عَزَّوَجَلَّ) stated:

وَإِذْ قَالَ ٱللَّهُ يَٰعِيسَى ٱبْنَ مَرْيَمَ ءَأَنتَ قُلْتَ لِلنَّاسِ ٱتَّخِذُونِى وَأُمِّىَ إِلَٰهَيْنِ مِن دُونِ ٱللَّهِ قَالَ سُبْحَٰنَكَ مَا يَكُونُ لِىٓ أَنْ أَقُولَ مَا لَيْسَ لِى بِحَقٍّ إِن كُنتُ قُلْتُهُۥ فَقَدْ عَلِمْتَهُۥ تَعْلَمُ مَا فِى نَفْسِى وَلَآ أَعْلَمُ مَا فِى نَفْسِكَ إِنَّكَ أَنتَ عَلَّٰمُ ٱلْغُيُوبِ. مَا قُلْتُ لَهُمْ إِلَّا مَآ أَمَرْتَنِى بِهِۦٓ أَنِ ٱعْبُدُوا۟ ٱللَّهَ رَبِّى وَرَبَّكُمْ وَكُنتُ عَلَيْهِمْ شَهِيدًا مَّا دُمْتُ فِيهِمْ فَلَمَّا تَوَفَّيْتَنِى كُنتَ أَنتَ ٱلرَّقِيبَ عَلَيْهِمْ وَأَنتَ عَلَىٰ كُلِّ شَىْءٍ شَهِيدٌ. إِن تُعَذِّبْهُمْ فَإِنَّهُمْ عِبَادُكَ وَإِن تَغْفِرْ لَهُمْ فَإِنَّكَ أَنتَ ٱلْعَزِيزُ ٱلْحَكِيمُ.

"**And remember when Allāh will say (on the Day of Resurrection): 'O Jesus, son of Mary! Did you say unto men: "Worship me and my mother as two gods besides Allāh?' He will say: "Glory be to You! It was not for me to say what I had no right to say. Had I said such a thing, You would surely have known it. You know what is in my inner-self though I do not know what is in Yours, truly, You, only You are the All-Knower of all that is hidden and unseen. Never did I say to them aught except what You (Allāh) did command me to say: 'Worship Allāh, my Lord and your Lord.' And I was a witness over them while I dwelt amongst them, but when You took me up, You were the Watcher over them, and You are a Witness to all things. If You punish them, they are Your slaves, and if You forgive them, verily, You, only You are the All-Mighty, the All-Wise.**" (5:116-118).

This is a refutation of the Christians who are being informed that Jesus will exonerate and free himself from them on the Day of Judgement. Allāh will ask Jesus about whether he invited the people to worship him and his mother as deities alongside Allāh.[72] Jesus will glorify Allāh and say that he had no right to say such a thing as it is

---

[72] The Qur'ān does not state that the Trinity consists of Allāh, Jesus and Mary. It simply states that Jesus and Mary have been taken as deities alongside Allāh which is factually true. Catholics invoke and worship Mary. A deity (ilāh), is that which is invoked and given devotion.

not from his qualities or rights to be worshipped, just as it is not the quality or right of anyone—be they angels, jinn or men—to be worshipped alongside Allāh. Jesus will state that he only informed them with what he was commanded to say, that he is a mere servant of Allāh, in submission and servitude to Him, and that the people should worship Allāh, who is his Lord and theirs.

The Non-Reliability of Previous Scriptures.

Previous scriptures, the Torah and the Gospel, have undisputedly suffered from loss, concealment, alteration, insertion and distortion over time and no longer accurately represent what Allāh revealed to Moses and Jesus (عَلَيْهِمَا ٱلسَّلَامُ), even if elements of truth can still be found in their current forms.

Rebuking the Jews and Christians, Allāh stated:

فَوَيْلٌ لِّلَّذِينَ يَكْتُبُونَ ٱلْكِتَٰبَ بِأَيْدِيهِمْ ثُمَّ يَقُولُونَ هَٰذَا مِنْ عِندِ ٱللَّهِ لِيَشْتَرُوا۟ بِهِۦ ثَمَنًا قَلِيلًا فَوَيْلٌ لَّهُم مِّمَّا كَتَبَتْ أَيْدِيهِمْ وَوَيْلٌ لَّهُم مِّمَّا يَكْسِبُونَ

"So woe to those who write the 'scripture' with their own hands, then say, 'This is from Allāh' in order to exchange it for a small price. Woe to them for what their hands have written and woe to them for what they earn thereby." (2:79). And also:

وَإِنَّ مِنْهُمْ لَفَرِيقًا يَلْوُۥنَ أَلْسِنَتَهُم بِٱلْكِتَٰبِ لِتَحْسَبُوهُ مِنَ ٱلْكِتَٰبِ وَمَا هُوَ مِنَ ٱلْكِتَٰبِ وَيَقُولُونَ هُوَ مِنْ عِندِ ٱللَّهِ وَمَا هُوَ مِنْ عِندِ ٱللَّهِ وَيَقُولُونَ عَلَى ٱللَّهِ ٱلْكَذِبَ وَهُمْ يَعْلَمُونَ

"And indeed, there is among them a party who alter the Scripture with their tongues so you may think it is from the Scripture, but it is not from the Scripture. And they say, 'This is from Allāh,' but it is not from Allāh. And they speak a lie against Allāh while they know." (3:78).

That the scribes and copyists took liberties, made alterations and inserted things from themselves, is empirically proven. For example, the verse in 1 John 5:7 is an established forgery, inserted in order to embed evidence into alleged scripture for the Trinitarian doctrine. There is compelling evidence that Matthew 28:19 has been doctored through injection of text within it, again to embed evidence for the

Trinity. The passage of Mark 16:9-20 (an entire twelve verses) is also a later insertion. Seeing that the end of Mark ends rather abruptly, the scribes improvised and "completed" the rest of the story. These three examples are not under any serious contention, they are proven and acknowledged insertions ("forgeries").

It is also known that the Pauline epistles—written by a man who never met Jesus—came well before the canonical gospels which were in turn written anonymously and later stamped with the names of "Mark", "Matthew", "Luke" and "John" at some stage in the second century. The Greek-speaking writers of the gospels introduced a pro-Pauline depiction of Jesus into their writings, leading to the hellenization and simultaneous dejudaization of Jesus.

The gospel of "Mark" contains errors regarding Jewish customs and habits. The writers of "Matthew" and "Luke" attempted to correct these mistakes when they copied "Mark" wholesale (92% and 54% respectively). Eye-witnesses would never need to copy the writings of others on such a scale and make corrections to them when they could simply write their own first-hand accounts. In "John", figurative, philosophical speech appears, mystifying and upgrading Jesus to a status not found in the earlier gospels.

Biblical scholar, Bart Ehrman writes: "The four Gospels... are all anonymous, written in the third person about Jesus and his companions. None of them contains a first-person narrative ('One day, when Jesus and I went into Capernaum...'), or claims to be written by an eyewitness or companion of an eyewitness. Why then do we call them Matthew, Mark, Luke and John? Because sometime in the second century, when proto-orthodox Christians recognized the need for apostolic authorities, they attributed these books to apostles (Matthew and John) and close companions of apostles (Mark, the secretary of Peter; and Luke, the travelling companion of Paul). Most scholars today have abandoned these identifications, and recognize that the books were written by otherwise unknown but relatively well-educated Greek-speaking (and writing) Christians during the second half of the first century."[73]

---

[73] Bart Ehrman in *Lost Christianities* (2003), p. 235.

Ehrman also notes: "Justin Martyr, writing around 150-60 CE, quotes verses from the Gospels, but does not indicate what the Gospels were named. For Justin, these books are simply known, collectively, as the 'Memoires of the Apostles.' It was about a century after the Gospels had been originally put in circulation that they were definitively named Matthew, Mark, Luke, and John. This comes, for the first time, in the writings of the church father and heresiologist Iraneus, around 180-85 CE."[74]

This is a well researched subject area and further details can be found in the scholarly resources listed at the end of this book.

The Qur'ān Clarified the Truth Wherein Jews and Christians Differed

Allāh (عَزَّوَجَلَّ) said:

ذَٰلِكَ عِيسَى ٱبْنُ مَرْيَمَ قَوْلَ ٱلْحَقِّ ٱلَّذِى فِيهِ يَمْتَرُونَ

"That is Jesus, the son of Mary - the word of truth about which they are in dispute." (19:34)

Allāh (عَزَّوَجَلَّ) also said:

وَمَآ أَنزَلْنَا عَلَيْكَ ٱلْكِتَٰبَ إِلَّا لِتُبَيِّنَ لَهُمُ ٱلَّذِى ٱخْتَلَفُوا۟ فِيهِ

"And We did not reveal the Book to you , [O Muḥammad], except for you to make clear to them that wherein they differed." (16:64).

The Islāmic message regarding Jesus (عَلَيْهِ ٱلسَّلَامُ) and the picture that emerges from research regarding the **historical Jesus**—as opposed to the **mythical and theological Jesus**—establishes the truth of that wherein the People of the Book differed.

Within that small percentage of what may be historically correct and accurate in the Gospels regarding Jesus is what agrees with the message and teaching of the Qur'ān regarding him. Hence, there are **two Christianities** embedded in the New Testament. The original *Jewish Christianity* which treats Jesus as a Prophet of God calling to faith, monotheism, righteous works and abiding by the law, and the innovated *Pauline Christianity* in which he is made divine. We shall take a look at the clearly discernable original in the next chapter.

---

[74] In *Forged* (2011), p. 226, citing Iraneus's work *Against Heresies*, Chapter 3, 7.11.

Jesus in the Gospels

The Qur'ān establishes that elements of truth still remain in extant versions of former revealed scriptures. It states that it came as a confirmation of past authentic scripture, clarifying what is true and false in that which is possessed by the People of the Scripture (*ahl al-kitāb*). It asks them to consider the Qur'ān:

وَهَٰذَا كِتَٰبٌ أَنزَلْنَٰهُ مُبَارَكٌ مُّصَدِّقُ ٱلَّذِى بَيْنَ يَدَيْهِ

"And this is a Book which We have sent down, blessed and confirming what was before it..." (6:92).

It invites them to believe in the Qur'ān and to accept the truth it has clarified for them:

يَٰٓأَيُّهَا ٱلَّذِينَ أُوتُوا۟ ٱلْكِتَٰبَ ءَامِنُوا۟ بِمَا نَزَّلْنَا مُصَدِّقًا لِّمَا مَعَكُم

"O you who were given the Scripture, believe in what We have sent down [to Muḥammad], confirming that which is with you." (4:47).

There are elements of the original true Gospel embedded in the canonical gospels of the New Testament that agree with the truth clarified in the Qur'ān regarding Jesus (عَلَيْهِ ٱلسَّلَامُ).

James Tabor, a scholar of the origins of Christianity and ancient Judaism, writes: "There are two completely separate and distinct Christianities embedded in the New Testament. One is quite familiar and became the version of the Christian faith known to billions over the past two millennia. Its main proponent was the apostle Paul. The other has been largely forgotten and by the turn of the first century A.D. had been effectively marginalized and suppressed by the other... Its champion was no other than James..."[75]

As has preceded, the actual gospel writers were evangelists and storytellers writing for their own audiences and being pro-Pauline they weaved a particular rendition of Jesus and his mission into the gospels. They deliberately omitted mention of the apostle James, the closest and most loyal of followers of Jesus and leader of "Jewish Christianity". Chronologically, one can see Jesus become more and

---

[75] In *The Jesus Dynasty: The Hidden History of Jesus, His Royal Family and the Birth of Christianity*. New York: Simon and Schuster (2006). p. 261.

more divine as we move from Mark to Matthew to Luke to John, this trend running parallel with the development of the Pauline Greco-Roman church as we move from the mid first to the early second century. However, these writers had to rely upon whatever was in circulation at the time regarding Jesus, his life and mission.

Research and analysis of the contents of the gospels reveal a common source referred to as "Q" which was most likely a copy or some form of representation of the original Gospel of Jesus. Inevitably, there will have been elements of truth in what those evangelists and storytellers ascribed to Jesus on the basis of such a source. Within these elements of truth, the message of Islām—*pure monotheism coupled with righteous works and observance of law*—can still be discerned.

At the same time, there were many other gospels in the hands of other sects, particularly the "Jewish Christianities". These sects were branded heretical and outlawed by the Pauline Greco-Roman church which dominated Christianity purely through the aid of empire and circumstance. These gospels were dismissed as works of heresy. These gospels would also have contained elements of the truth that have been lost. Because there is no empirically verified route of transmission from Jesus to the writers of the earliest manuscripts, it is not possible for Christians to speak about Jesus with certainty. In what follows, we present some truths that can be extracted from the canonical gospels and are known as such because they agree with the teachings of past Prophets, what can be found in the Torah and what is established in the Qur'ān.[76] Pauline Greco-Roman Christianity is an abrupt departure from the teaching of the Prophets and Messengers of old—monotheism, works and observance of law—and Islām is a direct reconnection to it.

Jesus called to Monotheism and Islām.

In Matthew 4:8-10 we read: «Again, the devil took Him to a very high mountain and showed Him all the kingdoms of the world and their glory. "All this I will give You, he said, "if You will fall down

---

[76] Refer to the book *Al-Barāhīn al-Injīliyyah* of Shaykh Taqī al-Dīn al-Hilālī and *Makānat ʿĪsā Fil-Islām* of Shaykh Rabīʿ bin Hādī.

and worship me." "Away from me, Satan!" Jesus declared. "For it is written: 'Worship the Lord your God and serve Him only.'"»

Jesus is cited in the Qur᾽ān as saying:

وَإِنَّ ٱللَّهَ رَبِّى وَرَبُّكُمْ فَٱعْبُدُوهُ هَٰذَا صِرَٰطٌ مُّسْتَقِيمٌ

"**And indeed, Allāh is my Lord and your Lord, so worship Him [alone]. This is a straight path.**" (19:36).

In Mark 12:28-32 we read: «One of the teachers of the law came and heard them debating. Noticing that Jesus had given them a good answer, he asked him, "Of all the commandments, which is the most important?" "The most important one," answered Jesus, "is this: 'Hear, O Israel: The Lord our God, the Lord is one. Love the Lord your God with all your heart and with all your soul and with all your mind and with all your strength.' The second is this: 'Love your neighbour as yourself.' There is no commandment greater than these." "Well said, teacher," the man replied. "You are right in saying that God is one and there is no other but him."»

This statement contains the declaration of Islām, which is to state that there is none worthy of worship except Allāh, and to serve Him by submitting to his Will through obedience to His command. He is only one Lord, one God, there being no other.

In Matthew 19:16-17 we read: « Jesus replied. "There is only One who is good..."» And in John 20:16-17 we read: «Jesus said to her, "Mary." She turned toward him and cried out in Aramaic, "Rabboni!" (which means "Teacher"). Jesus said, "Do not hold on to me, for I have not yet ascended to the Father. Go instead to my brothers and tell them, 'I am ascending to my Father and your Father, to my God and your God.'"»

It is interesting to note how in translation, the original meanings of Aramaic or Hebrew words have been upgraded and overwritten through interpolation in another language into words suggesting divinity. Thus, whereas Jesus is referred to as teacher, master, lord, son of God—all of which were clearly understood in the tongue of the Israelites—in the Greco-Roman rendition, Jesus is upgraded to Lord, Creator, Master, Son of God and aligned with mystery religion concepts involving human gods, saviours, sacrifices and redemption.

In Matthew 24:36 we read: «"But about that day or hour no one knows, not even the angels in heaven, nor the Son, but only the Father."»

Here, Jesus denies having knowledge of the Last Day and Final Hour. This is a denial of all-encompassing knowledge and hence an explicit denial of divinity on the part of Jesus. In the Qur'ān, Allāh states regarding knowledge of the Final Hour:

إِنَّ ٱللَّهَ عِندَهُۥ عِلْمُ ٱلسَّاعَةِ

"**To Allāh [alone] belongs knowledge of the Hour**" (31:34).

In John 6:38 we read: «"For I came down from heaven, not to do my own will, but the will of him that sent me."»

This is the meaning of Islām, to do the will of Allāh. This involves inward submission (*istislām*) and outward compliance (*inqiyād*) through observance of the law, something that Jesus evidently called to and which was faithfully enacted by his true followers led by the apostle James. This was rejected by the apostate Paul who abolished the law in addition to deifying Jesus.

Jesus Prayed and Supplicated to God.

In Matthew 14:23 we read about Jesus: «After he had dismissed them, he went up on a mountainside by himself to pray.»

In Matthew 26:39 we read: «Going a little farther, he fell with his face to the ground and prayed, "My Father, if it is possible, may this cup be taken from me. Yet not as I will, but as you will."»

Falling on the face is a reference to prostration (*sujūd*) and the Old Testament often makes mention of the Prophets such as Moses, Aaron and others falling prostrate on their faces, worshipping and invoking their Lord. This is the prayer of the Muslims who are the followers of the Prophets and Messengers in belief and worship.

And in Matthew 27:45 we read: «About three in the afternoon Jesus cried out in a loud voice, "*Eli, Eli, lemasabachthani?*" (which means "My God, my God, why have you forsaken me?"). »

This is according to the gospels, though Muslims do not believe or accept this. They do not believe Jesus was killed or crucified and nor do they believe that Jesus would speak with such blasphemy. But since this is in the gospel, it is a proof against Christians that Jesus is not divine. Rather, Jesus, as we see in other places, invoked his Lord and Creator in a time of need, thereby clearly distinguishing himself from his Lord. In Luke 23:34 we read: «"Jesus said, 'Father, forgive them, for they don't know what they are doing.'"» Here, Jesus invokes God to forgive those who do wrong. This establishes that he himself does not forgive sins thereby negating this divine quality from himself.

In Matthew 11:25 we read: «At that time Jesus said, "I praise you, Father, Lord of heaven and earth, because you have hidden these things from the wise and learned, and revealed them to little children."» Here, Jesus praises God who knows all things and reveals of them to whomever He wills and chooses.

In light of what has preceded, if Jesus prostrated to God, prayed to God, invoked God, praised God, asked for forgiveness from God, and stated there is only one Father, only One that is good, and only One who knows the Last Day and so on, it becomes clear that Jesus is a humble servant of God, a noble Prophet who taught people to be humble servants of God by following his example in worship and obedience. He denied divinity for himself. A human, by definition cannot be God and God, by definition, cannot be human.

Jesus's Confirmation of the Law.

In Matthew 5:17-20 we read: «"Do not think that I have come to abolish the Law or the Prophets; I have not come to abolish them but to fulfil them. For truly I tell you, until heaven and earth disappear, not the smallest letter, not the least stroke of a pen, will by any means disappear from the Law until everything is accomplished. Therefore anyone who sets aside one of the least of these commands and teaches others accordingly will be called least in the kingdom of heaven, but whoever practices and teaches these commands will be called great in the kingdom of heaven. For I tell you that unless your righteousness surpasses that of the Pharisees and the teachers of the law, you will certainly not enter the kingdom of heaven."»

In Matthew 19:16-17 we read: «Just then a man came up to Jesus and asked, "Teacher, what good thing must I do to get eternal life?" Jesus replied... "If you want to enter life, keep the commandments."»

Faith and the Necessity of Works.

In the Epistle of James 1:22-25 we find a clear confirmation of this teaching: «"But be doers of the word, and not merely hearers who deceive themselves. For if any are hearers of the word and not doers, they are like those who look at themselves in a mirror; for they look at themselves and, on going away, immediately forget what they were like. But those who look into the perfect law, the law of liberty, and persevere, being not hearers who forget but doers who act—they will be blessed in their doing."»

And in James 2:14-26 there occurs: «"What good is it, my brothers and sisters, if you say you have faith but do not have works? Can faith save you? If a brother or sister is naked and lacks daily food, and one of you says to them, 'Go in peace; keep warm and eat your fill,' and yet you do not supply their bodily needs, what is the good of that? So faith by itself, if it has no works, is dead. But someone will say, 'You have faith and I have works.' Show me your faith apart from your works, and I by my works will show you my faith. You believe that God is one; you do well. Even the demons believe—and shudder. You foolish person, do you want evidence that faith without deeds is useless? Was not our ancestor Abraham justified by works when he offered his son Isaac on the altar? You see that faith was active along with his works, and faith was brought to completion by the works. Thus the scripture was fulfilled that says, 'Abraham believed God, and it was reckoned to him as righteousness,' and he was called the Friend of God. You see that a person is justified by works and not by faith alone. Likewise, was not Rahab the harlot also justified by works when she welcomed the messengers and sent them out by another road? For just as the body without the spirit is dead, so faith without works is also dead."»

The apostle named James made it very clear that righteous works and obedience to God through faithful observance of the law is the way to God's kingdom, meaning bliss in Paradise. This was preached by the apostle James but rejected by the apostate Paul.

That salvation is through faith and righteous works, [after the grace and mercy of Allāh], is a matter that receives great attention in the Qurʾān and in the theology of orthodox Muslims who follow the disciples of Muḥammad (ﷺ) in their understanding of Islām, the Qurʾān and the law. In fact, when the doctrine of the removal of works from the reality of faith entered the Muslim nation, the disciples of the disciples of the Prophet (ﷺ) spoke against it vehemently and refuted it with the clear, explicit texts of the Qurʾān and the Prophetic teachings. Faith is what is in the **heart** of beliefs and emotions; what is expressed on the **tongue** of declarations, praises and thanks; and what is performed by the **limbs** of prayer, devotion and keeping commandments. This is a matter of consensus amongst orthodox Muslim scholars and is based upon a sound understanding of the revealed texts of the Qurʾān and the Prophetic traditions. Citing this consensus, the Muslim scholar, Abū Bakr al-Ismāʿīlī (d. 1059) said: "And they [the orthodox scholars of the Muslims] say: "Certainly, faith is speech (*qawl*), action (*ʿamal*) and belief (maʿrifah). It increases with obedience and decreases with disobedience. He whose obedience increases is more abundant in faith than the one who is less than him in obedience."[77] Those who opposed this doctrine were known as **the Murji'ites (the Postponers)** those who postpone deeds, or expel them from the reality of faith and they were of various groups, all united in their claim that deeds are external to the reality of faith and not an essential part of it.

Salvation through faith coupled with works is the religion of Jesus (عَلَيْهِ ٱلسَّلَامُ) and of James, the loyal upright companion, and of those with him, the pious predecessors among the Muslim followers of Jesus, just as Abu Bakr and ʿUmar (رَضِيَ ٱللَّهُ عَنْهُمَا) were loyal companions of the Prophet (ﷺ), firmly upon his way. This doctrine regarding faith and works clashes with the religion of the **arch-Murji'ite** and **Jahmite**, Paul (Saul of Tarsus), and the various doctrinal inventions of original sin, sacrifice and redemption which came afterwards under the influence of pagan mystery religions.[78]

---

[77] *Iʿtiqād Aʾimmat Ahl al-Ḥadīth*. Dār al-Fatḥ (1416H) p. 43.

[78] The **Jahmites** were a heretical sect that appeared in the early second century of Islām (early to mid 8th century CE). They asserted that mere acquaintance (maʿrifah) in the heart was sufficient for salvation, a doctrine in which lies destruction of faith and religion. Paul was a pre-Islāmic Murji'ite, inclined towards the Jahmite view, he abolished the law and made

God the "Father" and the "Sons of God".

It was known and understood that reference to God as "Father" and reference to men as "children" and "sons" of the "Father" is purely figurative and refers either to the relationship of *the Creator* to *His creation* when applied to all of humanity, or to the special relationship between God and the righteous, pious ones. This is clear and apparent in the Old Testament. Jesus is not exclusively singled out as a "son of God" and any such references should be understood in light of what has been mentioned.

In Matthew 5:9 we read the statement of Jesus: «"Blessed are the peacemakers, for they will be called *children of God*."»

In Matthew 5:45 there occurs: «"...that you may be *children of your Father* in heaven. He causes his sun to rise on the evil and the good, and sends rain on the righteous and the unrighteous"»

In Matthew 5:48 there occurs: «"Be perfect, therefore, as *your* heavenly Father is perfect."»

And in Matthew 6:1 we read: «"Be careful not to practice your righteousness in front of others to be seen by them. If you do, you will have no reward from *your* Father in heaven."»

In Matthew 23:8-9 we read: «"And do not call anyone on earth 'father,' for *you have* one Father, and he is in heaven."»

So in these texts we see God referred to as "*your* Father" and humans referred to as "*children* of God". The terms father and son refer to a relationship between the Lord and the servant and is used for righteous, pious people who observe the law.

In the 1906 Jewish Encyclopedia, under the entry of *Son of God*:

"'*Sons of God*' and '*children of God*' are applied also to Israel as a people (comp. Ex. iv. 22 and Hos. xi. 1) and to all members of the human race. Yet the term by no means carries the idea of physical descent from, and essential unity with, God the Father." And under the sub-heading, "The Pious as Sons of God" the entry continues: "... the title belongs also to any one whose piety has placed him in a filial relation to God... where 'the sons of God' are identical with 'the saints'... It is through such personal relations that the individual

---

salvation dependent upon knowledge and acceptance of Jesus's divinity and other heresies that neither Jesus, nor his followers knew of.

becomes conscious of God's fatherhood, and gradually in Hellenistic and rabbinical literature 'sonship to God' was ascribed first to every Israelite and then to every member of the human race."[79]

And under the entry of *God, Children of*:

"The Israelites are addressed as 'the children of the Lord your God' (Deut. xiv. 1)... As a man chastises his son, so does God chastise Israel (Deut. viii. 5); and like a father pities his children, so does God show pity... The relation of God to the individual man is also regarded as that of a parent to his child. 'For my father and my mother have forsaken me, but Yhwh taketh me up' (Ps. xxvii. 10, Hebr.; comp. II Sam. vii. 14). That other peoples besides Israel are God's children seems suggested by Jer. iii. 19."[80]

Jesus frequently referred to himself as the Son of Man in the gospels, a term that appears frequently in the Old Testament, particularly in the book of Ezekiel. In the Jewish Encyclopedia: "'*Son of man*' is a common term in the Psalms, used to accentuate the difference between God and human beings. As in Ps. viii. 4 (A. V. 5), the phrase implies 'mortality,' 'impotence,' 'transientness,' as against the omnipotence and eternality of God."[81]

To the Prophets of the Children of Israel and to the Muslims, it is impossible—rather, plain disbelief and pure idolatry— for God to be human or for humans to be God. The deification of Jesus took place within the pagan background of the Greco-Roman world in which gods were visible in the likenesses of men, walking on Earth. It was easy for a "son of God" of the Israelites, a pious worshipper, to become "*the* Son of God" and then "God the Son" just like Apollo—who represents the sun—was the son of Zeus.

Thus, in Pauline Greco-Roman Christianity, Jesus was framed for Gentiles in a way very much like the gods they already knew and

---

[79] The Jewish Encyclopedia (1906). 11/460. In . Genesis 6:2 there occurs: "...the sons of God saw that the daughters of humans were beautiful, and they married any of them they chose" and in Job 1:6 there occurs: "Now there was a day when the sons of God came to present themselves before the Lord, and Satan came also among them." And examples of this are numerous in the Old Testament.

[80] Ibid. 6/15.

[81] Ibid. 11/461-462.

worshipped. Jesus was moved from an Israelite monotheistic setting to a pagan, polytheistic Greco-Roman one. This must have suited the evangelists wanting to win converts from pagan backgrounds. This picture clearly emerges as we move chronologically from the earlier gospels to the later ones. In Mark (written around 70 AD), Jesus is least divine. As we proceed through Matthew and Luke (both written one or two decades later), Jesus is raised further, and finally in John (written around the turn of the century), we see Jesus as most divine. We see a transformation from a "Son of Man"—a clear negation of divinity—to the "Son of the Living God" and finally to "God" himself who came to dwell amongst men, the "Word" having become flesh, having eternally existed with God.

In the earlier gospels there is speech about righteous works and observance of the law as a means of attaining the kingdom of God; essentially **the beliefs and teachings of Jesus**. In the last gospel it is all about Jesus, who and what he is; essentially, **beliefs about Jesus**.

This evolution continued and through the influence of Greek philosophy, eventually led to the development of the Trinitarian doctrine over the passing of a few centuries. During the same time, the Pauline Greco-Roman Church declared those who maintained a non-divine or even less divine view of Jesus as heretics. Many writings that may have preserved much of the original Gospel were dismissed as heretical, banned, confiscated and burned.

Jesus Accepted as a Prophet and Messenger.

In Matthew 21:10-1 we read: «When Jesus had entered Jerusalem, the whole city was stirred and asked, "Who is this?" The crowds replied, "This is Jesus, the prophet from Nazareth in Galilee."»

In Matthew 21:45-46 we read: «When the chief priests and the Pharisees heard Jesus' parables, they knew he was talking about them. They looked for a way to arrest him, but they were afraid of the crowd because the people held that he was a prophet. »

In John 17:3 we read: «"Now this is eternal life: that they know you, the only true God, and Jesus Christ, whom you have sent."»

The earliest followers of Jesus, the so-called "Jewish Christians", were in reality Muslims in submission to Allāh, following the Torah and the Gospel. They took Jesus as a model and guide, seeking salvation through pure monotheism, righteous works and adherence to the law. They accepted Jesus as a Prophet and Messenger and knew that he was taught the Scripture, Law and Wisdom by Allāh. They understood that he was sent to them, the Children of Israel, to admonish and warn against sin and corruption and to invite them to righteousness and the immense reward that lies in the Hereafter, in the "Kingdom of God". They saw that he came to purify and confirm the Torah and to deliver them from the shackles of observance their leaders had invented and imposed upon them.

In the Qur᾿ān, Jesus is cited as saying:

قَالَ إِنِّى عَبْدُ ٱللَّهِ ءَاتَىٰنِىَ ٱلْكِتَٰبَ وَجَعَلَنِى نَبِيًّا. وَجَعَلَنِى مُبَارَكًا أَيْنَ مَا كُنتُ وَأَوْصَٰنِى بِٱلصَّلَوٰةِ وَٱلزَّكَوٰةِ مَا دُمْتُ حَيًّا

"[Jesus] said, 'Indeed, I am the servant of Allāh. He has given me the Scripture and made me a prophet. And He has made me blessed wherever I am and has enjoined upon me prayer and charity (zakāh) as long as I remain alive." (19:30-31).

This is just a small selection of texts from the gospels. Further research and analysis would reveal a lot more.

No Christian can be a true follower of the original teachings of Jesus except by following the truth brought by Prophet Muḥammad (ﷺ) and no Jew can be a true follower of Moses and of Jesus the Messiah whom he was supposed to believe in except by following Prophet Muḥammad (ﷺ) who came with a perfection of the Islām taught and preached by them both and by all the Prophets and Messengers. He also brought a complete law covering all aspects of life. This law is a confirmation and perfection of the Mosaic law, absent the shackles that had been introduced into it. It protects the human necessities of sound religion, life, property, intellect, lineage (material rights) and personal honour.

Anyone who desires and seeks the truth, opens his heart, researches, and then accepts Islām, knowing it is the truth brought by Moses, Jesus (عَلَيْهِمَا السَّلَام) and Muḥammad (ﷺ) will receive *a double reward*.

A Double Reward for Jews and Christians

Allāh (عَزَّوَجَلَّ) said:

ٱلَّذِينَ آتَيْنَاهُمُ ٱلْكِتَابَ مِن قَبْلِهِ هُم بِهِ يُؤْمِنُونَ. وَإِذَا يُتْلَىٰ عَلَيْهِمْ قَالُوٓاْ آمَنَّا بِهِ إِنَّهُ ٱلْحَقُّ مِن رَّبِّنَآ إِنَّا كُنَّا مِن قَبْلِهِ مُسْلِمِينَ. أُوْلَٰٓئِكَ يُؤْتَوْنَ أَجْرَهُم مَّرَّتَيْنِ بِمَا صَبَرُواْ

"Those to whom We gave the Scripture before it - they are believers in it. And when it is recited to them, they say: 'We have believed in it. Indeed, it is the truth from our Lord. Indeed [even] before it we were Muslims [submitting to Allāh].' Those will be given their reward twice for their patience" (28.52-54).

This verse is a reference to the People of the Book who believed in their prophet—Moses or Jesus—and then believed in Muḥammad (صَلَّىٰاللَّهُعَلَيْهِوَسَلَّمَ). For such Jews and Christians who accept Islām after having been faithful to the messages of Moses or Jesus there is a double reward for their patience. This is indicated in the authentic traditions. Prophet Muḥammad (صَلَّىٰاللَّهُعَلَيْهِوَسَلَّمَ) said: "*Three persons will receive a double reward*" and from them, "*a man from the people of the Book who believes in his prophet and believes in Muhammad.*"[82]

The scholars of Qur'ānic exegesis explain that this verse is a reference to Jewish Rabbis and Christian scholars who believed in their scripture and their prophet and then entered Islām. From them were ʿAbd Allāh bin Salām, a learned Jewish Rabbi from the tribe of Banū Qaynuqā, and Baḥīrā a Christian monk. When Jaʿfar, the Prophet's cousin, returned from Abyssinia after emigration to flee the persecution of the pagans, thirty-two Christian scholars who had accepted Islām came with him to the Prophet in Madīnah. Another eight Christians came from Syria, they were also leaders and scholars.[83]

These learned men recognized what their scriptures contained of prophecy regarding Muḥammad (صَلَّىٰاللَّهُعَلَيْهِوَسَلَّمَ) and were truthful to the covenant taken from them in their scriptures. After them, many others accepted Islām. The Companion Saʾīd bin Jubayr relates that

---

[82] Related by Imām al-Bukhārī.

[83] Refer to the tafsīr (exegesis) of Imām al-Ṭabarī, al-Qurṭubī and Ibn Kathīr by way of example.

he was amongst seventy priests that had been sent by Negus the Abyssinian king. When they came to the Prophet (صَلَّى ٱللَّهُ عَلَيْهِ وَسَلَّمَ), he recited Sūrah Yāsīn, the 36th chapter of the Qur᾿ān, from its beginning to its end. The priests began to cry and accepted Islām. The following verse was then revealed regarding them:

ٱلَّذِينَ ءَاتَيْنَٰهُمُ ٱلْكِتَٰبَ مِن قَبْلِهِۦ هُم بِهِۦ يُؤْمِنُونَ وَإِذَا يُتْلَىٰ عَلَيْهِمْ قَالُوٓا۟ ءَامَنَّا بِهِۦٓ إِنَّهُ ٱلْحَقُّ مِن رَّبِّنَآ إِنَّا كُنَّا مِن قَبْلِهِۦ مُسْلِمِينَ

"Those to whom We gave the Scripture before it, they are believers in it. And when it is recited to them, they say, 'We have believed in it. Indeed, it is the truth from our Lord. Indeed we were, [even] before it, Muslims [submitting to Allāh]'." (28:52-53).

Meaning that previously they were believers, they believed in the first Book (the Gospel) and then the second Book (the Qur᾿ān). For their patience upon the truth, they were given a double reward.[84] From the Christians who accepted Islām during the time of the Prophet was Negus (صَلَّى ٱللَّهُ عَلَيْهِ وَسَلَّمَ), King of Abyssinia.

Negus was the Christian King of Abyssinia, the Aksum empire—a region in present-day Ethiopia and Eritrea—and was described by Prophet Muḥammad (صَلَّى ٱللَّهُ عَلَيْهِ وَسَلَّمَ) as a righteous king under whose rule no one is oppressed. When the new converts to Islām were being tortured and oppressed in Mecca, the Prophet (صَلَّى ٱللَّهُ عَلَيْهِ وَسَلَّمَ) advised the Muslims to emigrate to Abyssinia. A small group of around fifteen emigrated in secrecy and this led the pagans of Mecca to increase their oppression and torture, angry that some Muslims had escaped from their clutches. A second, larger group of over 80 Muslims emigrated later, led by Ja῾far bin Abī Ṭālib, the cousin of the Prophet (صَلَّى ٱللَّهُ عَلَيْهِ وَسَلَّمَ).

After the second wave of emigration, the pagans of Mecca sent two delegates to King Negus of Abyssinia to convince him to return the Muslims to the Meccans. They argued that the Muslims were not upon the religion of the Meccans and nor the religion of Negus (Christianity) but had innovated a new religion and were nothing

[84] Refer to the explanation of this verse in *Tafsīr Ibn Kathīr.*

but fools and troublemakers. They also brought gifts for the King and his priests. Negus was a cautious and just man, so he decided to hear the view of the Muslims. He summoned them and asked about this religion which they were practising.

Jaʿfar bin Abī Ṭālib, representing the Muslims, said: "O King, we were a people of ignorance. We used to worship idols, eat [the meat of the] dead animal, we would perform shameless deeds, cut off the ties of kinship, ill-treat the neighbour and the strong amongst us would devour the weak. This is what we used to be upon until Allāh sent us a messenger from amongst ourselves. We know his lineage, his truthfulness, his trustworthiness and his chastity. He called us to single out Allāh [in His lordship] and to worship Him alone; that we abandon what we and our forefathers used to worship besides Him of stones and idols. He ordered us to be truthful in speech, to fulfil our trusts, to join the ties of kinship, to be good to the neighbour, to withhold from the prohibited sanctities and shedding of blood. He forbade us from shameless deeds, giving false witness, consuming the wealth of the orphan, falsely accusing chaste women [of indecency and lewd conduct] and ordered us to worship Allāh alone and not associate any partners with Him. He ordered us with prayer, obligatory charity and fasting and other affairs of Islām. So we attested to his truthfulness, believed in him, followed that which he came with, worshipped Allāh alone and did not associate any partners with Him. We treated as unlawful what Allāh made unlawful and we treated as lawful what Allāh made lawful. So then our people transgressed against us, they punished us and put us to trial with respect to our religion in order to make us revert to the worship of idols, away from the worship of Allāh, and so that we declare lawful what we used to previously consider lawful of vile things. When they subdued us, oppressed us, made life difficult for us and came in between us and our religion, we left our land and chose you over others. We desired your proximity and hoped that we would not be oppressed in your presence, O King."

When Negus heard this, he requested Jaʿfar to recite something from the Qur'ān and Jaʿfar read the opening verses of the nineteenth chapter, called "Mary" which recounts the story of Zacharias, John,

Mary and Jesus (عَلَيْهِمَاالسَّلَامُ). Upon hearing the Qur'ān being recited, Negus cried profusely until his beard became wet with tears and those around him also cried. Then Negus said, "Indeed this and what Jesus came with has emanated from the same lamp." Then Negus addressed the two delegates of the pagans of Mecca and said to them, "Be off! For by Allāh, we shall not deliver (these Muslims) to you."[85] Negus, recognising that Muḥammad was the one mentioned by both Moses and Jesus, later accepted Islām after the invitation of the Prophet (صَلَّىٰٱللَّهُعَلَيْهِوَسَلَّمَ). When hearing of his death, the Muslims performed the funeral prayer for him remotely from the city of Madīnah.

Scholarly research shows that the various "Jewish Christianities" and "Gospels" that existed in the early period after Jesus and which became obscure—being overshadowed by the spread of Pauline Greco-Roman Christianity because of the aid of empire—may have survived and not become completely lost. These communities may have moved and settled in various locations, remaining true to what they knew from their written records of the teachings of Jesus, believing him to be a Prophet and Messiah, sticking firmly to the law, and combining between inward faith and righteous works. These communities could have been the ones that accepted Islām because they recognised it as the truth due to their adherence to the true Gospel. They in fact saw themselves as those who were already Muslims due to adherence to the true Gospel. This also indicates that the Christianity known to the world today came to be because of the role of empire in its spread and acceptance, not because it was what Jesus and his followers were actually upon in faith and practice. This picture is now clearly emerging from the various detailed, rigorous studies published by scholars such as James Dunn, Bart Ehrman, Robert Eisenman, E.P. Sanders and others. These works are not written by Muslims but highly credentialed scholars and academics whose works are published by reputable academic publishers. Christians are advised to read these works with an open mind.

---

[85] Refer to *Rawḍat al-Anwār Fī Sīrah al-Nabī al-Mukhtār* of al-Mubārakfūrī (pp. 48-49).

Closing Notes

The true status of Jesus (عَلَيْهِ السَّلَامُ)—in between the neglect of the Jews and the extremism and excess of the Christians—has been presented. Jesus the Messiah, Son of Mary, was a righteous Prophet sent to the Israelites who preached monotheism and faithful adherence to the unadulterated Mosaic law which he came to purify and confirm. This teaching was carried and spread by his loyal disciples, at the head of them, James the Just.

The Qur'ān has clarified the truth to the People of the Scripture regarding Jesus and his status. They are obligated to respond to the Qur'ān and to the message of Muḥammad (صَلَّى ٱللَّهُ عَلَيْهِ وَسَلَّمَ) in which there is clarification regarding that wherein they differed.

The Prophet Muḥammad (صَلَّى ٱللَّهُ عَلَيْهِ وَسَلَّمَ) said: "*No Jew or Christian hears of me and does not believe in me except that he will be in the Fire.*"[86]

This authentic tradition shows that the message of Muḥammad (صَلَّى ٱللَّهُ عَلَيْهِ وَسَلَّمَ) is universal and not restricted only to the Arabs. The Qur'ān clearly addresses all of humanity in numerous places, and not just the pagan Arabs, Jews or Christians alone. It also indicates the abrogation of all previous revealed books and messages whose veracity and authenticity has been evidently compromised. There are an abundance of proofs establishing that the Qur'ān is revelation from Allāh.[87]

The above tradition also indicates—as Muslim scholars have explained—that whoever dies *without* hearing of Muḥammad (صَلَّى ٱللَّهُ عَلَيْهِ وَسَلَّمَ) and his messengership is excused on account of ignorance, though Allāh will test such people on the Day of Judgement. As for those who have heard of Muḥammad (صَلَّى ٱللَّهُ عَلَيْهِ وَسَلَّمَ) and his claim to revelation and messengership but do not seek to learn and grasp the reality of his message in an objective manner so as to ascertain its truth, then the proof is established upon them in the life of this

---

86 Reported by Imām Muslim in his Ṣaḥīḥ.

87 Fundamentalist and evangelist Christians have huge efforts in trying to discredit the Qur'ān as revelation from Allāh but they are handicapped largely by their profound ignorance of the Arabic language which is the purest of languages and closest to the mother tongue of all humanity.

world. Hence, it is upon every Jew and Christian, to *objectively* learn about Islām, upon a clean slate, devoid of any and all pre-conceived notions and biases built upon their present convictions and possibly a millennium full of lies found in antagonistic writings of religious leaders since the time of the Crusades which continue to shape and influence perceptions today.

As for those who deny the evident historical and revealed truths that have been highlighted and insist that Muslims are misguided and must become Jews and Christians, then the Lord of Moses and Jesus, the one who revealed the Torah and Gospel, has enjoined upon Muslims a noble and dignified response:

وَقَالُواْ كُونُواْ هُودًا أَوْ نَصَـٰرَىٰ تَهْتَدُواْ قُلْ بَلْ مِلَّةَ إِبْرَٰهِيمَ حَنِيفًا وَمَا كَانَ مِنَ ٱلْمُشْرِكِينَ. قُولُوٓاْ ءَامَنَّا بِٱللَّهِ وَمَآ أُنزِلَ إِلَيْنَا وَمَآ أُنزِلَ إِلَىٰٓ إِبْرَٰهِيمَ وَإِسْمَـٰعِيلَ وَإِسْحَـٰقَ وَيَعْقُوبَ وَٱلْأَسْبَاطِ وَمَآ أُوتِىَ مُوسَىٰ وَعِيسَىٰ وَمَآ أُوتِىَ ٱلنَّبِيُّونَ مِن رَّبِّهِمْ لَا نُفَرِّقُ بَيْنَ أَحَدٍ مِّنْهُمْ وَنَحْنُ لَهُۥ مُسْلِمُونَ. فَإِنْ ءَامَنُواْ بِمِثْلِ مَآ ءَامَنتُم بِهِۦ فَقَدِ ٱهْتَدَواْ وَّإِن تَوَلَّوْاْ فَإِنَّمَا هُمْ فِى شِقَاقٍ فَسَيَكْفِيكَهُمُ ٱللَّهُ وَهُوَ ٱلسَّمِيعُ ٱلْعَلِيمُ

"They say, 'Be Jews or Christians [so] you will be guided.' Say, 'Rather, [we follow] the religion of Abraham, inclining toward truth, and he was not of the associationists.' Say, [O believers]: 'We have believed in Allāh and what has been revealed to us and what has been revealed to Abraham and Ishmael and Isaac and Jacob and the Descendants [the twelve sons] and what was given to Moses and Jesus and what was given to the prophets from their Lord. We make no distinction between any of them, and we are Muslims [in submission] to Him.' So if they believe in the same as you believe in, then they have been [rightly] guided; but if they turn away, they are only in dissension, and Allāh will be sufficient for you against them. And He is the Hearing, the Knowing." (2:135-137).

All praise is due Allāh and may peace and blessings be upon the final Prophet, Muḥammad and all the other Prophets including those sent to the Children of Israel such as Moses, Solomon, David, Jesus and John.

Useful Scholarly Resources

Much modern scholarship is available regarding the *historical* Jesus in contrast to the *theological* or *mythological* Jesus. The research findings presented in the list of academic works below should be evaluated on their strength of argument and not dismissed merely because of the author or his personal beliefs.

1. Akyol, Mustafa. *The Islamic Jesus*. St. Martin's Press (2017).
2. Ehrman, Bart. *How Jesus Became God*. HarperOne Publishers (2014).
3. Ehrman, Bart. *Lost Scriptures: Books that Did Not Make It into the New Testament*. Oxford University Press, 2005.
4. Ehrman, Bart. *Lost Christianities: The Battle for Scripture and the Faiths We Never Knew*. Oxford University Press, 2005.
5. Ehrman, Bart. *The Orthodox Corruption of Scripture*. Oxford University Press (2011).
6. Ehrman, Bart. *Forgery and Counterforgery: The Use of Literary Deceit in Early Christian Polemics*. Oxford University Press (2012).
7. Ehrman, Bart. *Forged—Writing in the Name of God—Why the Bible's Authors are not Who We Think They Are*. HarperOne Publishers (2011).
8. Eisenman, Robert. *James the Brother of Jesus and the Dead Sea Scrolls I & II* Grave Distractions Publications (2012).
9. Eisenman, Robert. *The Dead Sea Scrolls and the Roots of Christianity and Islam*. Grave Distractions Publications; 2nd edition (2014)
10. Eisenman, Robert. *The Dead Sea Scrolls and the First Christians*. Element (1996).
11. Dunn, James. *Christianity in the Making Volume 1: Jesus Remembered*. Eerdmans Publishing (2003).
12. Sanders, E. P. *The Historical Figure of Jesus*. Allen Lane Penguin Press (1993).
13. Schonfield, H. *The History of Jewish Christianity*. Duckworth (1936)
14. Schoeps, H. J. *Jewish Christianity*. Fortress Press, (1969).